LOSE THE CAPE!

Volume 3

Ain't Nothing But a Teen Thang

D1569472

LOSE THE CAPE!

Ain't Nothing But a Teen Thang

edited by:

ALEXA BIGWARFE

&

KERRY RIVERA

KAT BIGGIE PRESS

COLUMBIA, SC

Ain't Nothing but a Teen Thang is the 3rd Book in the Lose the Cape! series. Learn more about all three books on http://losethecape.com

Cover Art: Adrienne Hedger
Interior Design: Write.Publish.Sell www.writepublishsell.co
Editing: Alexa Bigwarfe & Kerry Rivera

Published by Kat Biggie Press
Columbia, SC
info@katbiggiepress.com
http://katbiggiepress.com

ISBN 13: 978-1-948604109
Library of Congress Control Number: 2018907041
First Edition: June 2018

10 9 8 7 6 5 4 3 2 1

DEDICATION

To all you parents going through the teenage years, this too, shall pass.

In loving memory of Jon Haddock. 9/4/40 – 4/5/18

CONTENTS

Introduction ... 1

PART I: WHAT TO EXPECT...

Love Me, Love Me, Say that You'll Love Me
Alexa Bigwarfe ... 11

The Screen of all Screens
Kerry Rivera ... 17

Survival Years
Gretchen Kellaway ... 23

Tampons, pads, mood swings, oh my!
Tiffany Benyacko ... 27

Battling the System for Our Kids' Needs
Jeanine Lebsack ... 33

How to Love a Teenager
Nerys Copelovitz ... 39

Teenagers and Toddlers are the Same
Naomi Pelss ... 49

Just Listen
Janice Ricciardi ... 55

Parenting Hackers and Other Lessons You Never Expected
Summer Smith ... 61

Where did my sweet little one go?
Tash Warren-James ... 67

PART II: THE FUNNY

The Birds, the Bees, and the Fancy Money Snatchers
Echo Aspnes ... 75

Unintentional Insta-Spy
Leslie Blanchard ... 79

Vaseline®
Heather LeRoss ... 87

The Hair
Jennifer Rosen Heinz ... 95

Puberty: Just Around the Corner
Christina Surretsky ... 101

PART III: VALUES, TOUGH SUBJECTS, AND DIFFICULT DECISIONS

A Family that Plays Together
Katherine Mikkelson ... 109

This Mom Is Not Yet Rated
Danielle Silverstein ... 113

How to Raise a Feminist in 3 Easy Steps
Shanti Brien ... 119

Why I Said Yes to 5-Inch Heels for My 13-Year-Old
Jessa Vartanian Aubin ... 125

How to Equip Our Teens To Live A Godly Life
Christine Carter ... 131

Little White Lies
Shana Martin ... 139

PART IV: EXPERT ADVICE

Raising Lovable, Valuable, and Capable Teens
Lindsay Smith, LCSW ... 145

Navigating the Generation Gap with Co-Creative Communication
Laura Lyles Reagan ... 157

Parents, check your ego at the door to have a better relationship with your teen
Darren Horne ... 167

Keeping Teens Safe Online - A Prosecutors Perspective
Emily D. Baker ... 173

I Thought I was a Decent Parent until I had Teens
Jennifer Laurenza ... 183

Conclusion ... 189

Special Invitation ... 191

About the Editors ... 193

Acknowledgments ... 195

INTRODUCTION

As we write this book, my son is 11 years old. Solidly TWEEN. We're starting to have smells. Lots of smells. The other day, he and his friends played basketball in the hot South Carolina sun for about an hour. Then, they filed into his room to watch some YouTube. I stuck my head in at one point (to make sure they weren't looking at nudie pics) and nearly passed out from the smell. I told them they stunk and closed the door again. When I returned a little while later to announce dinner, apparently the Axe® body spray had made its way out, because now the room smelled more like a night club in Paris circa 1997. Once again, gas mask needed.

I wish it stopped at smells, but I am prepared for the fact that I am woefully unprepared for raising a teenage boy.

He's still my baby boy, but now we're talking about things that, honestly, I'd be okay NEVER having a conversation about. Like over dinner the other night, when he announces his friend "T" has changed this year, and *not* in a good way. I should have never asked *how?* But I did.

"Mom, 'Max' had to block him on Xbox because 'Troy' said he stuck his hot dog in 'Max's' mom's donut hole! 'Max's' mom said "Block 'Troy' now!'" Oh Good Lord. So, we're there ... already.

It was completely inappropriate on my part, but I laughed out loud. Mostly because I could imagine the expression on "Max's" mom's face as I imagined her screaming at her son to block the other kid. But I quickly realized I needed to stop laughing, because I didn't want my son to think this kind of talk was acceptable behavior.

But it continued to get worse... as I mentioned, we were sitting at the dinner table, and the two younger girls, who absorb everything, were listening intently. My six-year-old daughter quickly chimes in, "Why would anyone want a *hot dog* in a *donut hole*? Ewwww." I almost spat my dinner out. My husband abruptly changed the subject. Is this what life with a teenage boy will be like? Because as someone who grew up with three sisters, there was *no* talk about "hot dogs" or "donut holes."

I feel scared. Middle school—do we have to? I'm not prepared for this life stage. We've had emotional battle after battle. I'm not trained in the field of "how to avoid damaging your child." Over the years, I've learned to become a nurse, a personal chef, a chauffeur, a coach, a math and science tutor, a professional organizer and a party planner. I did not realize how much harder it would be to play psychologist/counselor. I mutter a lot to myself these days and then turn around and yell at my son for muttering under his breath to his teacher at school! I mean really, why on earth do we waste time learning Lamaze and breathing techniques? The medical professionals should be sending us to *psychology class* instead. It's more useful in the long run!

Right now I think I've truly found the 'sweet spot' of

2

parenting. The kids are old enough that they are self-sufficient and no longer mawling me all day long. They're still cute, sweet, and mostly respect us as parents. I feel like it can only get easier from here. Then I reflect back to an afternoon at my sister-in-law and brother-in-law's house about five years ago. Her kids were young teens. The conversation went something like this:

Me: "You have it so much easier than I do. I can't wait until my kids are a little bit bigger so that I can relax."

She practically snorted. "This isn't easy. It never gets easier, you know?" She was sitting by the edge of the pool. Her kids were off doing their own thing. No one had asked her to wipe their butts or get them a drink or get them the fiftieth snack of the morning. She wasn't a human jungle gym as little hands and feet crawled all over her. She was kicking back, enjoying an alcoholic beverage and, in my view, she didn't have a care in the world.

I thought she was crazy for insisting that life with teenagers could be as difficult as life with three little kids. I could barely keep my wits. My kids were six, four, and two, and I was *drowning* in motherhood. I didn't cope well with the constant neediness of these little creatures. The youngest was still potty training and I knew it would be years before she could independently go to the bathroom. The idea that it didn't get *easier* not only seemed unfathomable, but straight up depressing.

What I've learned as my children get older is that parenting comes in waves. The "hard" gets different. While they don't crawl all over me anymore or need me every two minutes, the worries and concerns are of a completely different magnitude. I no longer worry about one of them falling into a pool and drowning. Instead, I worry about them falling into the wrong crowd.

As I approach the teen years, my oldest child getting ready to begin middle school, I'm examining what life really looks like with teenagers. I see that my sister-in-law wasn't wrong. It doesn't get easier. It's just a different kind of stress. The emotional struggles and the difficulties of communication as my son becomes his own independent thinker are challenging and exhausting in a completely different way, and just as overwhelming. I'm terrified that I am not at all equipped to handle teenage children, and I'm relishing these years that I believe to be the "sweet spot" of parenting. They are still young and sweet and innocent, while very independent, able to entertain themselves and get their own snacks. They love and trust me. They are silly and enjoy being with me, and enjoy family walks, outings on the bicycles, and family movie nights. Their faces still light up with joy when they see me. My son is still happy that I come have lunch with him, even as a 5th grader. I'm terrified of what is to come as we turn the next corner.

It's not just a fear of the raging hormones and battles for independence. I fear for what the world has in store for our teens. While the technology access they have is incredible, it's also frightening. The stories of cyber-bullying, pressures of social media, the constant scrutiny of every decision, the things that they are exposed to —I'm sad for the loss of innocence and the maturing that has to happen too young.

My son sill seems like a little boy. But I know he's already being exposed to thoughts and actions that I wish I could shield him from for a few more years. Like "hot dogs" in "donuts." I am trying to prepare myself to help my son navigate the changes, both emotionally and physically, and I realize this period is not going to be easy. I know that we've done a good job raising our son, and I know that he'll make good decisions, but I would be lying if I didn't admit I am terrified about peer pressure, curiosities, the need to try it even though someone has told you not to do it, and then of course the "I know better than you" syndrome that all teens go through.

For those of you who have "grown up" with the *Lose the Cape* community, we wrote the first book when my oldest was in 1st grade and I had two toddlers. Kerry's oldest two were just a couple of years older than mine, but still in elementary school and she also had a preschooler. Life was different. Our worries and concerns were different. As our kids have grown, we've grown as parents as well. Still, this whole teen thing is different. We wanted to provide a book for other parents who are also transitioning into this point with their oldest child, and don't want to go it alone.

We've got your back! In this book, you're going to find stories, advice, a lot of different situations the parents represented in the book have come across with their children or remember from their days as teenagers. We come to you with our experiences and our history and our stories in the hopes that you will feel like you are not alone, and certainly not judged for the decisions you make. We do not come from a place of judgement, but in true *Lose the Cape!* spirit, we come in solidarity. We will survive this phase together too!

Likewise, we ask that as you read this, you refrain from

passing judgment on the decisions of the parents who have written these stories. We all make decisions based on our life experiences. It's not to be expected that someone's going to choose the same outcome for their children as you would choose for yours - you don't walk their path and they don't walk yours. This is one of the hardest lessons that I've learned in life—I can't expect other people to make the same choices and do the same thing as I've done because they don't have the same life experiences. They haven't been the places I've been. They haven't walked the journey that I've walked. They haven't had the losses that I've lost. They haven't been to the places I've been. Therefore, it's unrealistic and just quite frustrating to expect other people would act and behave in the same way.

However, there are some universal truths. We know our children need to be protected. So, we've included a section by legal expert and former public defender, Emily Baker, about protecting your children on the internet. We know communication is often a struggle with our teens, so we have a piece from Laura Lyles Reagan, a communications expert. And Darren Horne, who works as a mentor to teens every day, shares his advice on relating to teens and engaging with them in a more meaningful way. We also have input from a couple of licensed counselors and social workers, Jennifer Laurenza and Lindsay Smith, to help us with the emotional side of things.

It is our hope that these expert voices will give you some insight and help if you are struggling in these different areas. But the majority of the book is stories from parents currently going through this phase alongside with us or have recently made it to the other side. Some are funny, some not so funny.

We share different decisions we've made and why, in the hopes that you may connect with one or more of the stories and feel like you are not so alone.

We hope you laugh with us. We hope you love with us. We hope you nod your head in agreement and find some useful information and resources to help you parent your tweens and teens. And don't forget, you're already a super mom (or super dad!) without having to be Supermom!

With love,
Alexa Bigwarfe

PART I:

WHAT TO EXPECT...

THE PRACTICAL STUFF, MANEUVERING THIS STAGE OF PARENTHOOD, AND ADVOCACY

Is it just me, or did the book *What to Expect When Expecting* scare the bejeezus out of you? SO. Much. Information. Every little aspect that could possibly go wrong. Injuries and illnesses and so forth. And when I was done reading it, I might have felt less prepared to be a mother than when I started!

That's not what we're going to do with this section! In Part 1, we're talking about the practical stuff, learning how to maneuver this stage of parenthood, providing tips on advocating for our children, and helping them become little adults.

As our kids enter the tween/teen phase, we realize we still have boundaries to set and teaching to be done. We've also learned that some of the obvious stuff isn't always so obvious to parents. Like how to prepare them for their menstrual cycle, or ensuring they bathe frequently. These essays focus on helping you handle the "practical" things that can easily be overlooked because they are so second nature to us as adults. We also dig into what it's like to have to advocate for our children's needs and why we make the decisions we make to help our teens become little (although not always in size!) adults.

"ADOLESCENCE IS A PERIOD OF RAPID CHANGES. IN BETWEEN THE AGES OF 12 AND 17, FOR EXAMPLE, A PARENT AGES AS MUCH AS 20 YEARS!"

—UNKNOWN

LOVE ME, LOVE ME, SAY THAT YOU'LL LOVE ME
ALEXA BIGWARFE

I'm a little nervous about having the sex talk with my kids. My parents never talked to me about it. My mom simply said, "Don't do anything stupid that's gonna mess up your life."

Uh, okay. That was when I was 19, one year into college, and in a pretty serious relationship. Thank GAWD I was not the adventurous type in high school, because by the time I got this "lecture," I was beyond the point of needing it.

I had no brothers (so no males to observe) and three sisters, two of whom were quite a bit older, and a dad who was absent, not by his choice, from the time I was a young tween. There was no talk of love and relationships and safe sex. Needless to say, I don't feel like I have all the proper tools in my toolbox for talking to my children about love and relationships and sex.

As I thought about how I would prepare myself for this big event, I decided to practice with my nephew. (Cringe.) We were all in upstate New York at my in-laws for our annual summer family fun trip. My unsuspecting nephew was 16. One evening, as we ate dinner at the local bowling alley, he started talking about his girlfriend. I decided this was my moment.

"You know, T, girls, they are different than boys. When they become intimate with someone,"—his face got really red and he started squirming at this point—"they often become really emotionally attached. So just know two things. Don't go doing it unless you want that girl completely attached to you, and please use protection."

Nailed it.

At least I thought. He stood up, red-faced, murmured something like, "Um, okay, Aunt Lex," and got as far from me as he could. I don't think he talked to me again the rest of the trip.

Perhaps I need to hone my skills a little before I get into the land of the "talk" with my children. It's hard for me to imagine, but they'll be there soon. My son is 11. My daughter is eight. Some days I think my daughter is farther into the pre-teen mode than my son, but I can't stand the thought of either of them going down the intimacy road... for a long time. For many reasons. Heartbreak first. Stupid decisions second.

It feels like I should have years before I even need to broach the subject. But, if I think back on my own timeframe, I was 12 years old when I landed my first boyfriend in sixth grade. I remember when I started feeling those feelings. I stood on my balcony listening to my Dirty Dancing soundtrack on cassette tape as sweet Patrick Swayze crooned "She's like the wind..." staring off into the distance and hoping that the neighborhood cutie – Sven – would somehow find himself below my balcony to swoop me away. We lived in Germany at the time and I didn't care that he didn't speak English and my German was limited. The language of love would do the talking. But Sven never showed up under my balcony, and that's probably a good thing, because the rumors about him were that he was naughty.

Still, I had a plan B. Since I was fairly certain I would also not meet The New Kids on the Block that year and convince Joey-Joe that I should be his girl, I would settle for a boy in my class. Shawn. Shawn was dreamy. Hands down, the cutest kid in the sixth grade. And he kind of looked like Joey-Joe, with blue eyes and blonde hair.

I arranged the whole thing, with the help of my BFF, Angie. I wrote him the classic, "Will you be my boyfriend?" note.

He said yes and I was ecstatic. And surprised. I never imagined he would say yes.

I had no idea what to do next.

The next two weeks were pure terror for me. Every time I saw him headed in my direction at school, I went the other way. I literally hid from him for two weeks, which was challenging to do in our very small K-8 school on the tiny Illesheim Army base.

Then, the gauntlet dropped. Angie told me he would want to put his tongue in my mouth, and I was having no part of that. I had her deliver another note to him, indicating our relationship was done.

A week later, he and Angie were in a pretty tight relationship, and I'm pretty sure she let him put his tongue in her mouth.

I was young and innocent. My hormones were raging and I wanted nothing more than to be swept off my feet (or my balcony) by some love-craved fool. But I was shy. And thankfully so. Because if I had met a guy who showed me the right attention and got me alone and put on the moves, I don't know how

I would have responded. I was firmly in the "I'm waiting until marriage" camp, at least at that time, (um, hell, I was 12, not that that stops some girls) but no one ever tested that until I was much older and I knew what the heck was actually going on.

My parents sheltered me from everything, which was both good and bad. They never talked to me about anything important when it came to relationships and love and sex. Between my shyness and being terrified of any kind of intimate relationship, I avoided situations in which I might be pressured into doing anything I didn't want to do until I went to college.

But it wasn't for lack of want.

I wanted to have a boyfriend. I wanted someone to be interested in me. I wanted to feel loved. And I foolishly thought that love came from physical attention.

Now, I am raising two young daughters. I see the world through a completely different lens. While the idea of filling them in on the details of love and sex still terrifies me, the thought of them seeking approval and acceptance through sex scares me even more.

This becomes the moment when we have to decide – at what age are they old enough to know these things? I've decided it's definitely 12. At the latest. Because... Sven. And middle school. And access to all kinds of information, thanks to the internet we never had.

I saw a show on Oprah once about Rainbow parties. Ever heard of these? The girls put on different colors of lipstick, the boys put on condoms, and, well, the girls make a rainbow. You can guess where. The girls in this particular report were in seventh grade.

I'd love to be able to keep my daughters in a state of relative innocence until age 18 (or 25!), but I've come to realize I'd rather have them lose a little bit of innocence and gain some smarts to protect their bodies and hearts. Peer pressure is a bitch, and while I hope I've done all I can to give them the confidence they need to know it's okay to back away from situations that make them uncomfortable, I'm realistic about the ways of the world.

At least they'll know what happens when "Sven" comes along with all The Right Stuff. And if my talk of broken hearts isn't enough, I have a plan B. We're googling pictures of genital warts.

Alexa Bigwarfe is the mother of a tween son and two young girls. She is an author, a publisher, an author coach, podcaster, blogger, advocate for those without a voice, and social do-gooder. You can find her on Facebook at https://facebook.com/ LoseTheCape or https://facebook.com/WritePublishSellLLC. She writes about infant and pregnancy loss and grief on her personal blog, katbiggie.com . Alexa, her husband, three kids, and big dog live in famously HOT Columbia, SC.

THE SCREEN OF ALL SCREENS
KERRY RIVERA

When I discovered I was pregnant in the fall of 2003, I did what any rationale, first-time pregnant woman would do. Panic!

Yes, I was elated. Sure, I wanted to meet my little guy. Of course, I started buying clothes and nursery gear and tiny little baby goods.

I also grabbed books and parenting magazines, subscribed to Baby Center and scoured the web – because duh – I didn't know crap about being a mom. And I wanted to be a good one.

Beyond reading about breastfeeding and SIDS and cradle cap, I came across an article on screen time. It advised no – I repeat NO – screen time for kids under the age of two. No Sunday afternoon football in the background. No *Friends* in the evening. No *Baby Einstein*. Obviously. The noise, the colors, the motion, it would all scar the baby for life (or something like that). So, I printed out the article and photocopied it for my husband, the grandparents, the aunts, the uncles and the neighbors. Anyone associated with my precious boy had to read this article. In front of me. And vow NEVER to turn a TV on in the presence of my first-born son. Totally logical request, right?! The grandparents, especially, gave me a lot of eyerolls.

Fast forward 13 years and I've basically armed my kid with the screen of all screens—a smartphone. Why was I so obsessed about the TV in those early years? When I bought him an iPhone at the end of sixth grade, I set his life's journey onto a totally new trajectory.

Suddenly, he had access to YouTube and texting and online shopping. Oh, and phishing scams and porn and predators ...

I'm exaggerating. A little. Using my mad FBI skills, I added tracking and locked down inappropriate content. I also drafted countless rules about when and how he could use the device. Not in his room at night. Time limits during the day. No sharing his phone or passwords with others. We ensured only my husband and I could add apps via our passcode, and we check his browsing history and texts. So far, so good.

We bought the cell phone so my husband and I could communicate with him, but let's be honest ... my 13-year-old's texts are more like a series of letters.

IDK

Ya

No

K

Dinner?

At least I get letters. The text correspondence between his friends consists entirely of emojis. ☺

As a Gen X mom raising a Gen Z kid, this is new territory. Surely in 10+ years, the studies will reveal the negative impacts of giving a smartphone to a teen. In fact, I've already read a few. Point taken. #momfail

Every parent needs to make their own call on the cell phone debate. You decide when, the rules, the consequences. Like so many parenting matters, families will approach the topic differently.

For us, we opted to get my son a phone because he would be coming home to an empty house occasionally, and there are more and more events when he is getting dropped off and we bail. He's also a good kid. We'd been talking about phone use long before he got one, so he was clear on the expense and how anything he sends can get passed along—quickly.

I call it his "digital billboard".

Anything he texts, shares on social media or emails says something about him. If I saw it, would he be embarrassed? If his grandparents saw it, would he be worried? If his priest or teachers saw it, would he freak out?

If he can answer "no" to those statements, I tell him he is in a pretty good place. If he would say "yes," think again about the post. Nana or mama might hunt you down. #justsaying

My son is growing up in an entirely new digital age, and that's both totally awesome and terrifying. He can find images of beautiful places, create presentations within seconds and discover multiple points of view at every turn. On the other hand, the Internet and social media are not always safe places for impressionable tweens and teens – or me, if we're being real. The quest to create the perfect selfie – not so good. The cyber bullying is awful. And just the sheer amount of time kids can spend staring at a screen is harmful. Get outside. Talk to an actual person. Move.

I'm a worrier. Anyone who knows me, knows this to be true. I worry my kid will get swept into some awful Internet swell.

I worry he won't be able to hold a conversation with his reliance on texting.

I worry his generation will focus on online dating, instead of catching the eye of someone IRL.

I worry he'll think Tinder is a good way to meet people of the opposite sex – largely judging girls on appearances.

I worry he'll go blind from staring at a tiny screen for hours and hours in his lifetime.

I worry he'll focus on the number of "likes" and "comments" he gets with a post.

I worry he'll compare his life to someone else's immaculate online façade.

I worry he'll always seek instant gratification in a digital world that makes everything happen with a click or swipe.

I worry his device will be a distraction when he's driving, and he'll get in an accident, hurting himself or others.

I worry, but that's what moms do. I've got that part of the job description down. #likeaboss

My teen has had his phone for about a year now, and I'm proud to report he has not lost it, misused it or become addicted to the tiny screen that rules so many of our lives today. He still wants to ride his bike, reads actual books and has expressed no interest in acquiring a Facebook or Snapchat account. His texts with me are minimal, but I can reach him and he responds to my calls. We're doing OK.

In a few more years, we'll need to onboard another son, and then (gulp) a daughter. Not going to lie. Tackling the phone with a tween/teen daughter scares me to the core. The online viciousness I've seen with girls is beyond.

Who knows? The rules might change for them. As is the case with so many things, my first-born is the guinea pig. I research and obsess over the decisions we need to make, and then we take the plunge, adjust and I calm my crazy.

You can likely surmise that I eventually allowed the TV to be on in the presence of toddlers. I'm only human. I caved, and my three kids appear to be unharmed. Only time will tell the impact on our smartphone approach.

This is new ground for both of us. My first cell phone was a "brick" used only for emergencies, and I was 17. So, we'll navigate together, and remember to sometimes converse in person, smile and hug. #lovemyteen

Kerry Rivera's titles have ranged from journalist to PR Director to Digital Media Strategist, but in every role her primary goal is to tell her audience a story. Her career journey started in the newsroom trenches and has since transitioned to working for several large global brands. For many years, she managed her blog, Breadwinning Mama, where she delivered advice, musings and insights on juggling a full-time career and parenthood. She co-authored her first book - Lose the Cape - now available on Amazon, in 2015, and co-edited the sequel - Lose the Cape: Never Will I Ever (and then I had kids) later that same year. Kerry is mom to three kids and resides in Southern California, enjoying both the beach and mountains in her "spare" time. You can also find her at kerryrivera.com

SURVIVAL YEARS

GRETCHEN KELLAWAY

When my oldest child was born, almost 14 years ago, I knew absolutely nothing about motherhood, but I *knew* everything. I was a young mother, fresh in the trenches of maturity, a ripe 19-years-old myself. Everything I learned about being a mom, I learned from him. So, if I ever get a pat on the back for my skills as a mother, I usually point to my oldest and say, "He taught me everything I know." In the last 14 years, I have become a mother three more times, increasing my training, while relearning all the things I thought I already knew. Because the truth is, as a mother of four boys, I now know that "no child is the same." They all come with a new set of quirks and personalities. The second was a ball of energy, the third was a dance-to-his-own-tune kid, and my fourth—and final—is the boss.

So, back to my oldest, a few short months away from being a high school freshman, and still the old soul he was the day he started forming his personality. With him, everything was whimsical and magical. In those first few years it was just us against the world, learning the steps. Sunrises were beautiful and smelled of cinnamon toast and applesauce. I adapted to a life with less sleep, but also realized this motherhood thing is blissful, blessed, amazing. You can do anything. And I did. He was a fantastic toddler, so when his baby brother came along, I really thought I was prepared for this two-under-two thing. It wasn't horrible, but it wasn't easy. It was a whole new set of steps, a new schedule, and there were times I was sure I would never make it out. Yet, I did. I survived.

Now, I have found myself in a place where motherhood is just second nature. But, am I surviving?

I have teenagers, a tween, a grammar-school child and a toddler. My house looks like we just moved in, even though we've been here a decade. There is a line of dirt and grime up my stairway wall, ten years of growing handprints, like a back-yard art project. Toys are scattered everywhere and unfinished projects cover tables. It smells like dirty socks the majority of the time.

Our schedules are packed with Scouts and sports and kid-based activities. The moments I get to sit back and simply be me are very rare. I determined that eventually, the mess will be gone when my last child goes off to school. I reserve the cleaning for big holidays, birthday parties and when I just can't live in the mess anymore. I live on alerts, reminding me 30 minutes before we have to be on time for anything. I often feel like a drill sergeant, barking commands just to get kids moving into their shoes and out the door. Let's be honest; I often feel like I am failing.

And yet, I've managed.

How?

At 10, I teach all my boys how to wash their own laundry,

a chore that becomes their responsibility and later something that becomes a habit. Want clean socks? Do your laundry! It's worked. And now my oldest never has to say, "Mom did you see my soccer jersey?" because I didn't wash it. In fact, my teenagers are probably the reason I am surviving the last child. Without them getting themselves up for school, fed, and out the door without me leading the charge, I would probably still be a mom zombie.

Because my toddler is the boss, he often decides his bedtime, and generally demands all my time and energy. He is the center of my "mom universe" because he still needs me the most.

I have given my older boys the tools of responsibility to make my own life a bit easier. But I also know I'm sending them into the world knowing how to clean their underwear and cook something other than Ramen Noodles.

So that's how I began the journey of survival. Surviving by teaching them to survive without me.

All my firsts have been accomplished with my oldest. It's hard watching him grow up, and I have to witness these stages with each son. Survival is hiding tears. It's wanting them to want to cuddle with you one more time, knowing you embarrass them a little when you want one more hug at school drop-off. Survival is that last diaper, bottle, good-bye kiss.

It's knowing that mornings are no longer filled with cartoons, but rather the constant treasure hunt for lost shoes and lost papers. It's knowing that soon, you will be healing broken hearts and dealing with the stress of college choices and the realness of "What do you want to be when you grow up?"

The tools I give my teenagers might seem simple, but raising human beings is hard.

Life as a mom is fast-paced and always moving. It's like trying to wade through a swiftly moving river when you are weighted down and constantly pushed back. It hurts. A lot. Eventually though, you get to the other side, you reach dry land, and you survive the teenage years. I feel bruised, but I survived, and I can celebrate. The toddler is the river. Inexhaustible.

I don't pretend to know it all. I know nothing. I am not a genius at motherhood, I am not some saint, just an everyday woman, winging this whole thing and hoping that at the end of the day I gave my boys the tools to survive.

Gretchen Kellaway is a mother to four boys who lives in a small New Jersey city. She writes for therapy, to get her soul out with words. She takes inspiration from her family, her life struggles and her children. A lifelong love of reading and creative arts has melded to make her who she is today. When she isn't writing, or nailing this motherhood thing, you can find her about her community with Scouts. You can find her on Facebook at https://www.facebook.com/Momof4BoysBroken/ and Instagram @gigikway

TAMPONS, PADS, MOOD SWINGS, OH MY!

TIFFANY BENYACKO

I was 12, 6th grade, on the playground at school (yes, back then 12-year-olds still played on actual playgrounds!).

I felt something down below but wasn't quite sure what was happening. I turned my head to look at the back of my pants. A little surprised by what I saw, I took my jacket and tied it around my waist.

It was happening! I could not wait to get home to tell my mom. When I got home and told her she gave me a pad and sent me on my merry way. I wasn't prepared for this, the start of my period, and as a mother now, I realize how much more my mom could have done to help me when the day arrived. Here's my list of suggestions to help mothers prepare their girls for the "big day."

Have bite-sized versions of the "talk."

My daughter is at the onset of this whole puberty thing. It's been hard to have conversations with her about puberty without the mention of sex (eek, I said it!). The decision to discuss sex is up to the parent, but realize that your child will hear about it elsewhere. Don't you want them to hear a version closer to the truth than some far-fetched version from their friends? Yes, it's a touchy subject, but take a deep breath and prepare. You may be surprised at how much she already knows, so these types of topics are best handled in small bites. You really want this to be a conversation where the two of you are asking each other questions, having an ongoing dialogue; this is not a lecture. This is definitely a topic where you want to be honest and open with your tween girl.

Casually discuss bodies.

Tweens don't necessarily like discussing their bodies with their parents, so tread softly. From time to time, they may mention hair growing in places where it's never grown before. Take your opportunities as they come; don't be pushy. Once the opportunity presents itself, use yourself as an example. What did you do when you were her age? How did it make you feel once your breasts started to grow? When did you start growing armpit hair? The key here is to let your tween know that what's happening to her is normal.

It's important for her to know the correct name for the parts of the female reproductive system and how each part functions. Knowing your own body should not be viewed as taboo or nasty, it's your body! Girls should be encouraged to learn their own bodies.

Explain the menstrual cycle.

No worries, you'll have to explain it again ... and again ... and again. Most pediatricians say that once a girls' breast buds start to appear, her menstrual cycle should start a year later. It also depends on the age a girl's mother was when she started her cycle. Either way, start talking about it before it shows up!

Visit the feminine hygiene aisle at your local stores.

Don't make it awkward by specifically going to the store to visit the tampon aisle. Your weekly Target runs are perfect! Just casually stroll over to that aisle and point out a few things, like the maxi pads or tampons. You are sure to get questions about how they look, what to do with them, what's the difference between the two options and which ones you use.

Once you are home, explain the purpose of pads and tampons and how to use them.

Which will she prefer? Explain how to use each item. Pads are easy to explain, tampons ... well.

If you're in full teacher mode, there are great websites that explain and show how to insert tampons. Visit the sites together. Afterward, if she hasn't hit the floor, keep the conversation going by suggesting that pads are still an option. As she gets used to monitoring her cycle, she can determine which option fits her best.

Make sure she already has a hygiene routine in place.

Puberty brings with it body changes, which results in body odors and/or facial irritations. As parents, we must make sure that they have the necessities for a daily/nightly routine, which includes soaps for bathing, lotion for their bodies, facial cleanser, and a moisturizer.

Explain why she must use the hygiene products.

Having a good hygiene routine helps for when she starts

her period. There may be instances where her period stains her clothing, or when she will need to change her pad. It's nothing to be embarrassed by, but it's important to have certain items to stay as fresh as possible. Of course, it will take time for her to adjust to these changes and become skilled in using hygiene products, but we all seem to master this stage eventually.

Put together a "refresh" kit for her to carry in her backpack.

A refresh kit is a bag/pouch that holds extra maxi pads, clean underwear, at least two pain relievers, and wipes. It can be kept in her backpack or purse and is always ready for when she needs it. Let her know that her "refresh" bag will need new items added once she starts her period - spare underwear, pads, ibuprofen, or something similar.

Keep her yearly physical appointments.

Sometimes kids need to hear certain things from other people aside from their parents. Yearly physicals can be a time when your daughter can ask the doctor any questions about her changing body. She may feel more comfortable in asking the doctor certain questions.

Get the books.

"The Care and Keeping of Us" has become a staple between moms and their girls. I purchased this set because it comes with separate books for moms and their daughters, as well as a journal.

Read the books.

There is a difference between having the books and actually

reading them. Read the books separately and together. Another reason why I like "The Care and Keeping of Us" is that it allows us to share reading time together and gives my daughter an opportunity to ask me questions. Having separate books also gives us the space to go off and read if we'd rather be alone.

Commit to being honest with your daughter.

Before the rubber hits the road, settle this within yourself: you will be honest with your daughter about things that will happen to her body over the next few years. Decide on how you will phrase certain things, how you will back off when she doesn't want to talk to you. Realize that you are there to give information; this is not about you controlling her. Put yourself in her shoes. Remember what it was like? Yes, you and I turned out ok but let's not deceive ourselves; times are different. I know that every generation takes pride in saying this but c'mon, we didn't have social media. Nuff said!

Know how to de-stress.

Even though my daughter and I have been having our conversations on puberty for a while now, I am usually drained at the end of each and every one! A part of me struggles with not wanting to tell her anything, in hopes that she will stay 10 forever. Then reality sets in and I realize that I MUST have these conversations with her before she starts googling it or listening to her friends.

So to avoid or lessen being drained after these conversations, make sure that you have ways to take care of your mental needs. Trust me, you will need an outlet.

Whew!

It may seem overwhelming, but it's needed and worth it. Your daughter is off on this journey of puberty, which isn't a one-size-fits-all type of topic. It should be diced into bite-sized conversations, repeated frequently, and come from you, the parent. Having a period is just part of the journey.

Strap in, Mama, you're on one of the most important road trips of life with a daughter!

Tiffany Benyacko is writer and mentor, who uses her authentic voice to reach parents struggling to coparent. Being divorced herself, Tiffany realizes that people get divorced for many reasons, which probably includes them not getting along. With such conflict, coparenting can be challenging. For this reason, she uses her experience to advocate for shared parenting alternatives when coparenting does not work. Her work has introduced many parents in the United States and abroad to parallel parenting, a form of shared parenting for high conflict parents. As a result, many have found confidence in creating and executing parallel parenting plans that fit the needs of their families. Tiffany blends her writing on parallel parenting with raising a prepubescent tween girl on her blog, Unrehearsed. Her work on both topics has been featured on the Huffington Post and several parenting and divorce online journals. Tiffany is a Georgia native where she resides with her husband and daughter.

BATTLING THE SYSTEM FOR OUR KIDS' NEEDS

JEANINE LEBSACK

Editor's Note:

Advocacy for our children is one of the most important roles parents play. This essay demonstrates just how difficult that continues to be, even into the tween and teen years. For all of you parents who are dealing with appointments, the medical system, the healthcare systems, struggling to get diagnoses, struggling with medicine, and battling the system so that your kids can have the best support and best quality of life, you TRULY ARE super heroes. This beautiful essay provides coping mechanism from Jeanine, who has two sons on the spectrum and is truly an advocate, but gets tired, too.

"Well why don't you just let him fail?" I stared in disbelief at this person, one of the many "professionals" in our world of many doctors and specialists. Shocked, I simply responded, "I can't, and I won't. He's my son and he needs me."

This conversation occurred when I was seeking an ADHD diagnosis for my son who was already told he had Oppositional Defiant Disorder (ODD) and anxiety. The psychiatrist assessed him, and said ADHD and ODD tend to go hand-in-hand and the pediatrician didn't agree with him. Thus, a long journey began to try to help my son. If you think just entering the teen years is difficult, try doing it while also battling the health care system and advocating for your child.

This particular doctor made the growing list of "people with a white coat I wanted to punch in the throat!" My son was suffering, and I felt powerless. I was told my son's inattentiveness and impulsive behaviors were due to pre-adolescence and hormone related. HORMONES! I mean, we all know entering the tween/teen phase is hard enough, but this was more than hormones, and this doctor was not helpful. Meanwhile, I have a child so wound up with anxiety and a brain that just won't slow down; he can't sleep or eat properly. This is not hormones. Cue the sleep-deprived-going-to-lose-my-ever-loving-mind "Mombie" screaming at the top of my lungs for somebody to help me help my son! I knew there was something more to what was happening with my son—I just had to find someone to believe me. The people on our medical support team didn't know my child as well as I did. They didn't spend day-in and day-out observing his behavior. So, I set out to prove them wrong.

It took three years of assessments, follow-up phone calls, emails, dietary changes, and finding a new pediatrician, but he finally got the ADHD diagnosis. Now we're able to get medication and resources to help, but there is still a lot that has to be managed on the home front, especially now that he is almost a teenager. The oppositional behaviors turned my son into someone I don't recognize or like and are more than difficult to handle. I needed help. It's difficult to share, but I think any parent of a special needs child understands the difficulty in raising our children with different brain wiring. There is always love though, even if sometimes it has to be tough love to keep him in line. When his anger rages, it's his little brother who has autism that can set him off like a firecracker. They each have a sensory disorder -- one avoiding sensory input and the other seeking it. It's a difficult balancing act some days; my home can quickly become a battle front as I have to intervene when the two different personalities and sensory spectrum collide.

Throw in the added hormones of becoming a teenager, and we're bound to have some rough moments ahead. I believe what my children need from me is to love, accept, and respect them. We all have bad days and those lead to bad moments.

I'd like to share some of my coping mechanisms with those of you who are also parents of special needs children and feel alone and lost and don't know how to get through.

First, it's normal to feel anger. Anger at the medical system, anger at life, anger at God, even sometimes anger at your children. Just remember, they're children and they can have stressful and anxious feelings too. I'm human and my feelings get hurt but it won't do anyone any good if I indulge in them. I dig deep to find the strength to pause for a breath, pray, and seek help from any parental and neurological source I can find.

Don't over complicate the situation. Your child needs straightforward direction and routine. The K. I. S. S. method (keep it simple, silly) give short and simple instructions. First, then, after are steps that can be broken down easily and help with executive functioning. Because the ADHD brain can be so easily distracted and chaotic, I have had to invest a lot of time in teaching organizational skills to my son, a must in middle school. First my son gets the assignments written in the school agenda and the homework sheets come home in the backpack. At home we have a white board where the assignments are written on and we attach the homework sheets with due dates highlighted. Before we even attempt homework, I prepare a snack as I know a nourished belly helps to feed the brain as well. And he won't be able to focus on homework if he's hungry.

Knowledge is power, so arm yourself with as many sources of information as you can. With ADHD and other similar conditions, there are some challenges and issues with the executive functioning in the brain and it's important to break instructions down into a way they clearly understand. Clear communication is the cornerstone of our family, not only with my son but with the whole family. A year and half ago his brother was diagnosed with autism and a rare genetic disorder called 16 p11.2 proximal duplication. We need a lot of help when it comes to emotional regulation and staying focused. And it's okay to realize you can't do it on your own and you need help. We're well-versed in the Zones of Regulation, a program to help children handle emotional control and self-regulation. I highly recommend parents with special needs children to look into this program at http://www.zonesofregulation.com. Another resource I recommend is the Alert program, that helps children stay centered and focused. (https://www.alertprogram. com/) We are not afraid of learning about methods of therapy that may seem unusual to other parents. We discuss ways to help with self regulation such as deep pressure massages, skin brushing/joint compressions, weighted blankets, and essential oils—all tools in our inventory for self-care. These help when the world's closing in and causing too much sensory overload for our sensitive souls. You'll be amazed at the resources you can find to help when you're willing to explore different options.

Don't be afraid to talk about it. We talk a lot about the brain and its functioning in our family, so discussing the ASD and ADHD happened naturally. I guess my son has an advantage because I understand what he is experiencing. I was a child with ADHD and didn't get a diagnosis until recently, so I am able to share with him but you don't have to also be diagnosed to discuss what is happening inside their brains with them. And you'll learn some fascinating tidbits. The most interesting fact that I learned is the genetic factor. One doctor told me ADHD was more hereditary than heart disease! That gave me the wake-up call to get past my wondering of 'why me?' and seek my own path to assessment.

Love them authentically, even when the hormones and their conditions get the best of them. Raising two boys - one with ADHD and one on the spectrum and (awaiting an ADHD diagnosis) and with all kinds of "letters" to learn about is about is not easy. Entering the teen years has only added to that craziness.

Life has knocked me down more times than I can count but I get back up and I persevere. Living in the alphabet soup has taught me more resilience than surviving high school! It has given a purpose to understand myself and my own labels to better help my children. I know my kids respond best to me simply and authentically loving them.

Failure is not an option.

Jeanine is a busy special needs parent of two awesome sons. She advocates for mental health, rare diseases, and autism spectrum disorder. She's a proud hockey-loving Canadian who spends her spare time in hockey arenas cheering on her favourite player— her oldest son. She also loves making up silly songs with her superhero youngest son. Reading and writing are her passion and she's determined to finish her book and see it in print before her kids are driving! She couldn't do any of this without the strong arms of her husband and his love and support. You can follow her journey here: https://jsackblog.wordpress.com

HOW TO LOVE A TEENAGER

NERYS COPELOVITZ

Remember when your snarly, gangling tween was a wee babe?

They were so easy to love. That oversized head with the big googly eyes, those chubby thighs, that intoxicating smile.

Even during the terrible twos, and the question-packed threes and fours (help!), there were moments of sheer unconditional love—and not just when they were asleep :)

It was so easy to wonder at their marvelousness: their budding personalities, their newly found abilities, their adorable observations.

Secretly, we even liked their naughty side too, (though heaven forbid you let them know that), because it showed gumption and character.

But mainly they were just so cute—and they adored us in return, mostly anyway.

But your tweenage daughter?

The one who rolls her eyes because "you don't get it." The one who slams her door because "I hate you." And the one who snarls when you dare suggest her t-shirt is a little too revealing for a twelve-year-old. Now she is not so easy to love.

And that man-boy who grunts at you like a caveman, smells like a buffalo, and empties your fridge with alarming efficiency? That pimply, self-absorbed, know-it-all is just plain harder to appreciate.

They change moods and personalities—from BFF to the Devil's twin and everything in between—with such frequency that we never know what to expect.

Sometimes it's easier to keep a safe distance, stand on the sidelines waiting and praying for this to pass. Or we may "go to battle," fighting at every turn to maintain control and respect, trying desperately to find the adorable child we had... whilst pushing away the emerging teenager.

But wait, it doesn't have to be this way.

As the mother of two teenagers and one budding tween, I've been in the front lines for almost a decade, and here's what I've learned...

Your tween or teen needs you more than ever—but in a different way.

They need you to back off, but stay close.

They need you to communicate—mostly by saying nothing.

They need you to stay calm, but stay on the ball.

They need you to be warm and emotional, but expect nothing in return.

Confused?

Your tween/teen surely is. But you needn't be. Read on for what it takes to love your teenager.

#1 Get informed, become empathetic

Remember how, when you were pregnant, you read a lot

about what was going on inside your body. And how, during the first year, you were probably guided by some kind of "manual" on what to expect and how to deal?

Go there again.

When my first child reached fifth grade, he shot up overnight, like a spring bud erupting from the earth on fast forward. His voice dropped, his appetite doubled, and his eyes started avoiding mine. It felt like I was suddenly parenting a totally different child.

Exactly then, I ran across an ad for a parent education course: "Keeping the Channels of Communication Open with Your Teenager."

It was a gift from heaven. This "Adolescence 101" taught me the essentials about teenage brain development, the evolutionary need for teens to 'rebel' and 'separate,' and the pressures of being a teenager in the world of social media, soft drugs, and accessible alcohol.

More than anything, it made me feel *empathy* for my child and what he was going through, and because of that I could love him more easily through the changes (when he was not always at his best).

Here are some great resources to help you understand what adolescence is all about:

Untangled: Guiding Teenage Girls Through the Seven Transitions into Adulthood by Lisa Damour. Untangled explains what's going on, prepares parents for what's coming, and lets them know when it's time to worry.

Ahaparenting.com. Aha! Parenting is authored by Clinical Psychologist and renowned Parenting Coach, Dr. Laura

Markham. Her relationship-based parenting model teaches compassionate, common-sense solutions which will bring your teen closer.

#2 Show love, build their self-esteem

When your kids were little, you'd greet them with a huge hug, smother them with kisses and call them "sweetie" or "honey." You praised them for the most menial things and boasted about them to anyone patient enough to listen.

Your teen does not want that—**but secretly needs it** (they'll never admit that though).

Despite their adolescent prickles, and the fact that most of the time they seem NOT to want much to do with you at all, they badly need to be loved, praised, and hugged.

There are plenty of non-invasive ways you can express your love to your big kids, without embarrassing them:

- The obvious—tell them you love them. If it's hard for you to vocalize, send a text or emoji, and say it with your eyes and your tone.
- Greet them with enthusiasm (even when they just grunt at you in return).
- Learn the art of foot, hand, or neck massage, and offer a pampering 10-minute "treatment."
- Find something positive to compliment them on every day – even the smallest things like "I'm so grateful that you got out of bed and went to school today. I know you don't always feel like it."
- Spoil them occasionally by doing the unexpected: tidy

their room, make them a special dinner, buy them a small present, offer to host a sleep-over or pizza-fest for their friends.

#3 Become a listener, stay connected

Many teenagers stop talking to their parents, claiming "you don't understand" and "you're not listening to me."

Or they feel their parent's disapproval and disappointment, and so chose not to share their experiences, including how school is going.

It's true that some kids, especially girls, talk more, but even quiet kids need to off-load their worries. And yes, teenage boys do talk...

Here's how to do it:

Where: Teens often talk freely over food, that's why a regular family meal is so important. But in addition, take them out one-on-one for their favorite food and a chat. Car journeys are another great opportunity. Something about the privacy and minimal eye contact helps them to "confess."

How to get them talking: Don't bombard them with questions. If a conversation doesn't start naturally, tell them something that happened to you recently, (sharing a problem or something goofy that you did is a great way to get them to lighten up). Or talk about a TV program, sports event, the news, or family members.

Most importantly: When your teen talks, just listen. Make eye contact, keep your expression as neutral as possible, nod your head or "uh huh" occasionally, but DO NOT offer advice or pepper them with questions. When they finish talking, try to summarize what they've told you with a "So let me get this right..." or "So I understand you're..." and let them respond. Only then, ask if they want your opinion or advice (and if they don't, tell them that's okay, and that you're available to listen anytime.)

Trust me on this one.

Learning to listen without passing judgment or giving unwanted advice, will radically improve your relationship, (and this goes for any relationship), and make your teen feel accepted and understood. That way they are more likely to come to you when they DO need help or advice.

Here's a great book to help you out on this:

How to Talk So Teens Will Listen and Listen So Teens Will Talk by Adele Faber. If you didn't catch this book when your kids were young, it's not too late to integrate its legendary method into your parenting toolbox.

#4 Have realistic expectations, keep it positive

With perfectly good intentions, many parents would like to have indefinite control over their child's life. They want to keep them safe and help them become successful. But adolescence is all about establishing independence from our parents and that comes about through a process of separation.

Your tween may not want to come with you to visit their grandparents.

They may not want to take part in your family movie nights anymore.

They'll prefer to go to the mall with their friends.

They'll be less tolerant of younger siblings and need more privacy.

That's normal. Adjust your expectations and get your teen to cooperate with events that are important to you by including them in the planning process, or by making it easier for them to say yes (adding food to the equation is always a winner).

Key "conflict areas" are:

- Sleep - If you know your teen likes to sleep in late at the week-ends, don't schedule a trip for 9:00 a.m. (or at least don't expect them to jump with joy when you do).
- Chores - When you ask them to do their chores, let them do it when they finish watching a program, or at a set time.
- Appearance – Respect their need to experiment with their hair, clothing, and mannerisms. This is part of their search for identity.
- Tidiness – Shut the door on their untidy room so it bothers you less. Set an agreed time (weekly, every two weeks) when they'll empty their trash, pick up clothes and return plates to the kitchen.
- School – Make sure your teenager knows how highly you value education. Give them all the help they need/want to make Middle and High School bearable. Don't ruin your relationship with your child over grades.

#5 Cut the disparaging talk; respect and accept

I hear so many parents belittling their teenagers—whether

it's constant nagging or criticizing, making negative put-downs (often in front of others), comparing them with more successful children, or harping on about how they've got it easy compared to how you had it.

Then they wonder why their child is withdrawn and hides in their room.

Yep, many kids today are "spoiled" compared to their parents' childhood. Yes, teenagers are often uncooperative and unfathomable.

But negative talk will only make that worse.

We all need to vent about how hard parenting is, and how worried we are about our kid (and whether they are normal!). Talk to your spouse or empathetic friends who have children the same age or older than yours. You can also visit internet sites and forums to get support and read how you are not alone in your struggles.

Losethecape.com is a place for busy moms to find encouragement and advice about how to cope.

#6 Don't take offense; model emotional maturity

When you have a teenage child, you will often feel offended.

They'll make you feel outdated, uninformed, slow-witted, ungainly, incompetent, and sometimes just darn old.

But you mustn't take it personally.

It's not about YOU.

Suck it up. Laugh it off. Cry it out. Whatever works for you.

You are the adult here, and your reaction needs to be considered and mature, not childish and retaliatory.

And take note, when something hurts you, it's probably because there's an unresolved issue. Our kids make us face our open wounds—providing us with an opportunity for healing and personal growth.

#7 Be a safe harbor and they'll always come home

If your tween/teen feels understood and loved, if they know you'll listen, if you have mutual respect, and they know your reactions will be considered, they'll be less likely to be defiant, less likely to make bad decisions, and more likely to come to you when they need help.

You'll be their safe harbor. An unmoving solid rock of safety and love in the stormy sea of adolescence. That's what they need.

At the end of these turbulent years (and even before then), you'll fall in love with your teenage child again, in the same crazy way that you loved them when they were a baby, because they will become remarkable adults, due in a large part to all your hard work. But don't go expecting any thanks!

Nerys is mom to two gorgeous teenagers and one devilish nine-year-old. Being a parent has made her heart soften and her eyes shine (often with tears of frustration) and is way the hardest, but most rewarding, job she's ever held. You can follow her at https://www.facebook.com/nerys.copelovitz

TEENAGERS AND TODDLERS ARE THE SAME

NAOMI PELSS

I am a 43-year-old mother of four children. At this stage in my life, I have a toddler and a teenager (and two boys in-between). Parenting a toddler and a teenager at the same time can prove exhausting, and quite difficult. (On a related note, I have never consumed so much wine in all my life.) However, raising a toddler and a teen at the same time has given me a great perspective on these two stages of development. I can see many similarities between a toddler and a teenager. In fact, they are so similar I can apply the same parenting techniques to both children. I consider this quite a blessing as I will look for any shortcut to make parenting in my forties a little easier.

The Top Ten Ways Toddlers and Teens are the Same

1. Toddlers and teenagers are emotional.

That seems like an understatement. They have huge emotions that can burst from them at any time. It's like a heavy rain that comes in quickly and lashes down for several minutes. As their parents, we have to ride out the storm. No umbrella can fully shield you from the downpour. Please note that just like the weather, these emotional outbursts cannot always be predicted. There will be raging storms, but there will also be days of pleasant sunny times with little-to-no chance of rain. We all soak in the sun on those days.

2. Toddlers and teenagers fight to exert their independence with every breath they take.

They are adamant they don't need you. They want to do things for themselves. They are struggling to figure out their world. We must allow them enough freedom to try and try again, make mistakes, and master the skills they so desperately want to learn. We must stand back and just watch at times, restraining ourselves from doing it for them, and refraining from saying, "I told you so".

3. They eat a lot and they like to sleep.

Feed them. Let them sleep. Good luck when they are both tired **and** hungry at the same time. Sometimes I picture a hibernating bear that was rudely and prematurely awakened from a deep slumber. Do not go near the grumpy bear! Just throw some food at it and let it go back to sleep! Back away slowly, keep your distance, and you will be safe.

4. Teenagers, like toddlers, have incredible tantrums. Although I often want to join them in their fits of rage, yelling, screaming, foot stomping and door slamming, this behavior is not recommended. Don't get sucked into the drama. As mentioned in #1, just ride out the storm.

5. Both toddlers and teenagers can be very territorial and self-centered.

The toddler mantra is "me, my, mine". The teenage mantra is "selfie, selfie, selfie." It's all about them. Be reassured this is a stage they will outgrow. As they are learning to love themselves, they will learn to love others just as much. Keep role-modelling unselfish behavior.

6. They like to watch videos. Internet videos seem to be popular for both.

Annoying music, movies, or videos of people who make them laugh will satisfy both a toddler and a teen. Just make sure you are watching from the eyes in the back of your head. There are videos we do not want our toddlers *or* our teens to watch.

7. They say "No!" a lot.

They tell me to "Go away!" I thought at first my toddler learned this phrase from his teenage sister, but I think it is just innately part of their toddler/teen vocabulary. We must try not to take it personally. What they are trying to say is that they need some space. Remember, we could all benefit from some time alone.

8. They are incredible to watch when you are not with them. I see them when they are without me.

They act like different people around their friends and other people. I like to watch my daughter in dance class when she is fooling around with her friends. She is so happy and free and silly. I am reassured that toddlers and teenagers have many moods and they are not always a ticking time bomb waiting to explode.

9. They grow overnight.

One morning my toddler had a toe sticking out of his footy pajamas. He honestly busted through the feet during one nap. My teenage daughter is the same. She is growing so fast we can hardly keep her clothed. Teenagers don't just hang out at the mall because they like it. I think it is out of necessity. At any minute now they grow into the next shoe size and need new ones immediately.

10. They both need love now more than ever.

They think they don't need you, but they do. Keep on loving them even when they are at their most difficult. Let them know that you will always be there for them. Listen to them when they talk about things that matter to them. Try to connect with them on their level. Toddlers and teenagers are a lot alike and parenting at these stages is an emotional roller coaster for everyone involved. Keep calm and parent on (and stock up on wine).

It's the end of a long day and the busyness of my toddler has left me exhausted. I am giving him a bath to get him ready for bed and thinking about rewarding myself with a glass of wine. I glance at a photo on the wall of my teenager when she was a baby and realize in the blink of an eye it is going to happen again. It seems like one minute you are bathing a baby, and the next minute she is all grown up. One minute I was watching princess movies with her and I was her whole world. The next minute I was taking her and her best friends to the movies and walking around the mall alone because she does not want to be seen with me.

I feel time slipping away right before me. I desperately scoop my little one up and hug him as I inhale that intoxicating smell of a freshly bathed and towelled baby. I bring him downstairs to where my teenage daughter sits on her smartphone. She makes a funny face at him and he giggles and runs to her with open arms. She is so kind and loving and wonderful to him.

She understands him and all his emotions and now I realize just how connected they are. They are in some ways, the same. They are just trying to make sense of the world they are living in. They want to feel grown up and powerful. They feel deeply about everything and it bursts from their bodies in unbridled emotion. My heart swells as I realize my first toddler turned out to be a pretty great teenager and I have a feeling my next one will as well.

Naomi Pelss is a wife and mother of four children ages 13, 12, 8 and 2 (a toddler, a teen and two red-headed boys in-between). Her youngest blessing came when she was 41 years old. Naomi has a degree in Child Studies but admits there is a lot more to learn about children. She has been a registered Early Childhood Educator for almost twenty years and is now a Kindergarten educator. She blogs about her parenting journey at www. morewithfourblog.com Some of her posts are informative, some are sentimental, and some of her posts are funny. All of her posts are honest and real.

JUST LISTEN

JANICE RICCIARDI

Well, I can never go back to that Starbucks. After the barista twice asked me if I had an "outie," I abandoned all civility and snapped, "What is wrong with you? Why would you ask me that?!"

Wounded, he replied, "I just thought we had the same car," gesturing to the Audi key in my hand.

With this came the crushing realization that I don't listen. My barista was equally culpable; every week I give him my name and every week he writes "Jazz" on my cup. I am inappropriately buoyed by the fact that he sees me as someone interesting enough to have the name "Jazz." But when we recover from our awkward encounter, I order and I listen to myself. Sure enough, I pronounce my name like I am recovering from a stroke. This propels me to question my ability to listen, to myself and others, in my life outside this Starbucks.

My newly minted teen is quick to say I don't listen to her. Oh, but I do. I am just so often afraid of what I will hear, because it means my adoring little sidekick is growing up and away from me. Straight into the arms of Channing Tatum. Or maybe Drake. And I want to roundly reject this idea. It's hard enough to let her go. But how do we listen when we don't want to hear echoes of our own unhappiness at this age?

Suddenly, her thoughts no longer perfectly align with my own. The horror. Why, oh why, did I encourage her to question authority? Not mine. I meant: start a second-grade petition to take "Stuffies" out to recess. I am mourning the loss of her babyhood, hoping to stuff a kid with bigger boobs than me back into a Baby Bjorn. Instead of paying attention to the young woman she is becoming, I am unfairly stifling her by instructing her to remain the guileless, sweet girl she was when she was seven. I need to stop trying to quiet the emotional crashing that is necessary to her development. She is her own as a person—not me.

Methinks I doth project too much. There may be a connection between her growing up and my hypersensitivity to what I hear. Suddenly, her innocence, and my ability to protect her, is threatened and everything I hear becomes obscene. When puberty struck in sixth grade, I irrationally shrieked at the pediatrician with the slight lisp, "Next time you ask my 11-year-old about school, you may want to tag the word 'grade' onto your inquiry so it doesn't sound exactly like you just asked her, 'So what do you think about SEXth so far?'"

When she was safely wrapped in my infantilizing arms, I didn't listen so closely. In fact, I blithely ignored that niggling inner voice that cautioned, Is your kindergartner's Halloween costume really a "bunny ballerina?" Or are you sending a 5-year-old to school dressed as a Playbook Bunny? Because really, what's the harm?

But now the harm feels huge and predatory. I know adolescence is another normal stage, but it feels so much more dangerous: sex, technology, drugs. This is not the stuff of potty training and lisps. Those I had a fair amount of control over; I knew the outcome. This stage can so easily go wrong.

So I scramble to protect her. I try to preemptively fix it all for her, to give her advice that comes out as barked orders. And I forget to listen. This is not a working strategy. I know that if I don't start really listening, she's going to stop talking. Conversation is suddenly stilted as I try to penetrate her teen force field. The pressure to be more interesting than Instagram is enormous. As we talk about the stress of her day, I imagine "Lean on Me" building to a tear-jerking crescendo as I mother her, in an award-winning way; only to realize there is a booming silence as she surreptitiously sends a pic on SnapChat. Where did I lose it?

My role as mother to a toddler was so clear. Perhaps I enjoyed it so much because I had seeming control; a stranglehold on the wonderful simplicity of little kids. When they adore you. When you are the smartest, funniest, most "oh-sum" mother.

I did not anticipate this slow slide into an insular decade of head-down mothering. It was not so many years ago that 9pm would find me slapping on a fresh coat of Vamp, ready to go out dancing. Not writing kids' names on bananas with Sharpie and vetting the American Girl® book about periods. I intended to do this and remain vivid in the larger world. But as she blooms, I feel myself fade. Her growing up is accelerating my plunge into middle age, and I am not doing this gracefully. While I love that she wants to borrow my Rolling Stones concert t-shirt, her referring to it as "vintage" makes me feel like a wizened biker chick reliving her Altamont days. Accepting her growing up is to accept my own growing older and out of the world of full-time mothering. Into a stage of mothering that scares me.

My peers tell me I have it pretty easy, that the climate with their teens can be icy. Around here, it's not the hate, it's the humility. It's so hard to allow the person who peeled open my heart and taught me about joy to also step away from my wildly clutching arms. To accept that I cannot fend off every hurt or disappointment she will face is humbling and horrible.

Giving her the benefit of my experience and perspective is not working out as I planned. I hear myself imparting Maya Angelou-worthy nuggets of wisdom. My advice is not well received. Not that it's ineffective, it's just so misguided: nobody wants that shit. I so desperately want her to heed my counsel. But she hears: "I've vetted some of the riskier ones, and here are some thoughts for you to think."

I have to stop throwing up roadblocks on her path to independence by trying to fix her teen ills. After all, she can't skip the messiness of adolescence and launch straight into well-balanced adulthood. I forget that she really is listening and learning how to navigate her own thoughts, her own life. Hell, I'm not that well-balanced an adult anyway. I am learning that refusing to listen will not stop time.

I have to listen now. My daughter, as a tiny, controllable little being, has gone away.

I should have seen this change coming. I somehow didn't know I'd miss the detritus of Cheerios and glitter. That her dolls "Puffling" and "Roast Beef" would be packed away. Now I see the boobs and braces. My hair is blown back by the spiraling moods. My heart; cleaved by her squirming away from my touch aches for her hyper self-awareness.

With this change comes an uncomfortable shift in the supply and demand of motherly love. When she was little, it seemed so draining. Yet now, as her demand dries up, I find myself with an aching surplus. And it is throwing into chaos my identity. My adoring little girl is all I know, and I've got my role down pat. More than ever, I realize to stay connected, I have to shift into a new role. I have to listen.

While I celebrate her burgeoning independence and intellect, I am loathe to disavow her of her childhood innocence. As I try to preserve our bond, I am flailing around trying to figure things out in my new role. I see my peers accommodating their tweens' developing maturity by relegating themselves to second class citizens. They take them to movies but are banished to sit three rows away. They respond to vitriolic screaming with measured responses like, "Nevertheless, you may not have an iPhone." They allow themselves to be demeaned and disrespected in the guise of "encouraging individuality." I reject this new role.

We are both between worlds. Caught between child and adult, she faces starting her period while still clinging to her love of Santa. It's confusing for both of us. Yet she is also a thoughtful, quick-witted, sweet, whip-smart young woman. I already adore her more than any roommate I ever had.

And so, I should stop stifling a shrieked, "I forgot to cherish it!" and revel in the spectacular changes and delightful tween who is emerging. Thinking I can choose the right, new role for myself before actually living it with her is absurd. As is the notion that this is the hard stuff; we haven't even entered the real arena of teenaged-girl yet.

Maybe by the time my younger daughter is a teen, I'll have gotten this listening thing right. I'll stop jumping in and start trying to really hear her. I'll be a little more "Jazz," and a little less crazy and controlling. But my skewed listening reared its head tonight. Revelation: When your seven-year-old reads from a Disney Fairies book and, inexplicably, drops the final "n" from words, a book featuring lots of "barns" and "horns" sounds exactly like Bukowski.

But I must stop hearing threats, and creating fear, in every stage of my daughters' development and try to listen. I practiced with the little one tonight when she announced, "I only sleep with black guys." My eyes widened in surprise, but I sat back and listened as she clarified: "I don't want these stuffies with blue eyes, just the ones with black eyes."

I might hear a lot, if I stop and listen.

Janice Ricciardi is an exotic Canadian, married to a New Yorker, raising daughters in San Francisco. She used to talk on the radio, but now finds herself writing kids' names on bananas with Sharpie and vetting the American Girl book about periods. She has been featured in Parents Magazine and on scarymommy. com, greatmomentsinparenting.com, mommyish.com, TheMid.com, Popsugar.com, and inthepowderroom.com.

PARENTING HACKERS AND OTHER LESSONS YOU NEVER EXPECTED

SUMMER SMITH

After having four children relatively close in age, I felt I could say with some level of confidence that the most important trait one needed to possess to succeed as a parent was patience.

When your children are toddlers, patience is a recurring theme. It seemed a reasonable leap to assume this character trait was the hardest skill I would need to master in order to mother at the highest level and take me through the remaining years with ease. This call for patience comes when we are forced to repeat the most mundane of tasks and reiterate acceptable methods of interacting with siblings and friends—over and over.

Sadly, most of us realize very quickly that we do not naturally possess as much patience as we thought we did, and that moment is a humbling one. The early years are hard, and while I believe we mean well when we cross paths with that young and tired mother at the park or grocery store check-out line, and utter the words, "It gets easier," I think it might be less helpful than we realize.

We often say it with such sincerity that I think a little part of us wants to believe that it's true. Here's the reality I could have never expected while expecting, parenting never runs on auto-pilot, and it never gets easier. The things that stretch us simply take on new forms, but there is always a call for diligence and instruction that never allows our work to be done. Each season is filled with its own set of unique challenges.

After residing for so many years in the little-kid stage and becoming a master of my craft, I found myself marching rather confidently into the tween years. Sure, it's a season of burgeoning hormones, comprehending consequences, and the pushing of boundaries, but I had patience down … so I was totally ready for the tween scene.

The biggest reality check during my parenting shift into this season came when I was confronted with the truth that my once chubby-cheeked toddler who was expected to listen to my every instruction; had suddenly transformed into an opinionated pre-pubescent child, who wanted to make all of their own choices and was quite certain I was out of touch with the mainstream.

The challenge comes when our teens do in fact make some of their own choices, and their selections are not only different from the ones you would have made, but occasionally turn out to be disappointing, misplaced, or selfish. Classically these choices result in a series of natural consequences. In other moments, we are forced to dole out our own allotment of intentional consequences in an effort to turn the misstep into a teachable moment.

During these moments of instruction, it is easy to lose sight of the bigger picture as we find ourselves swept up by the undercurrent of our own emotions. We might inadvertently direct our frustration toward our spouse rather than working with them to solve the problem together. We might yell or overreact, or worst of all say things that can't be taken back in the presence of our children. The reasons why can widely vary, but in those moments, we reveal our more flawed adult persona rather than our quality parent one, and it is easy to become discouraged.

Then it happens, and we are faced with a moment requiring our parental attention, and the pieces fall perfectly into place. We unite with our partner as virtual masters of instruction. We come up with a punishment that fits the crime. We use the moment to teach a valuable life lesson that we ultimately were not aware our child was ready to learn, until it became apparent that they were. We seize the conflict with sage-like wisdom and transform an unfortunate situation into something for good. In these moments we are parenting at the highest level, and it feels amazing.

I recall heading to bed one evening and performing a last-minute sweep of my emails. It was then that I discovered my son had cracked my very elaborate password, and the breech meant unauthorized purchases had been made on his gaming account. Going to bed I realized there were things that had not been specifically spelled out for my child ... like don't be a hacker, and don't steal money, and these things were going to need to be addressed. The offense was disappointing, but it was manageable, and a teachable lesson would certainly follow in the morning.

The next day I found my inbox flooded with a string of additional email receipts. The offense was bigger than I had initially thought, and his father and I were required to hold a disciplinary council meeting. We talked calmly. We formulated a plan. We sat our son down and spoke to him on the topics of trust, money, and how things don't just magically appear with a click from the great iCloud in the sky.

The determination was that had he asked to make some money we would have found jobs for him to earn funds. Because he instead took money without permission, he had to pay us back... with interest. The punishment took weeks to complete, and in many respects felt a little like I, as his supervisor, was also being punished. We pressed on, and the underlying lessons were reiterated every single day. "Where does money come from, son?" I would ask. "It comes from hard work and over time," he would reply. It was a mantra, and we chanted it daily for nearly three weeks.

Ironically, the punishment wasn't the hardest part of the entire process. The part that came next in my opinion was surprisingly more challenging. In our varied social exchanges, I'm sad to say it, but people often disappoint us or do not meet our perceived expectations. The result of this interaction causes many of us to become list keepers. We log offenses into an imaginary note book we keep tucked in our back pocket. Moving forward this little black book impacts how we choose to interact with people. We decide how much of ourselves we will now give them, and what kind of boundaries we will ultimately set with those individuals based on a series of exchanges we've logged in our book of transgressions.

The bottom line is if you have experienced conflict with someone...you simply elect to limit your time spent with them. Sure, we say that we forgive the offense when a contrite individual comes to us to ask for our understanding, but in reality we don't forget how the circumstances made us feel. The offense in question always stays with us in some form, and every time we see that other person it whispers to us.

When you fast forward to our role as parents, and the fact that there is an entire decade where we are tasked with walking beside an individual with our genetic flaws and shortcomings rooted into their very DNA, who make mistakes daily, our call to navigate the element of forgiveness is not as simple of a task.

As much as we thought patience was difficult to achieve, the ability to instruct, forgive, and still maintain intimacy with our developing child is perhaps the most challenging aspect of parenting. Forgiveness is not our default setting, for we are an easily offended society, and as a general rule find the very act goes contrary to our own survival.

Despite what seems an otherwise improbable task, I believe it is in the very act of choosing forgiveness over bitterness where we find its greatest personal blessing manifested in our lives.

The forgiving component is more for us, than it is for our offspring's benefit. When we make this necessary shift in our perspective, we come to find the very failures, disappointments, and lessons they must navigate serve not as marks to enter into a book of their transgressions, but as necessary growing pains for their souls.

When we see the circumstances for what they really are, character shapers, then our new perspective grants us the clarity to move beyond the moment of unmet expectations and see only the child, and the person we desire for them to ultimately become.

What I never expected when I was expecting was just how hard it is to raise a quality person, but even more than that just how much motherhood would in fact teach me. I now realize there is no one magical quality that we are called to master as parents. However, when we as individuals evolve right alongside our child through the ever-changing seasons, we too will experience the blessing that comes from perseverance.

Ultimately, our call is to remember we are writing a choose-your-own-adventure story with our children, and the best stories are always filled with the most colorful of characters, and the most unexpected plot twists.

A native of the Pacific Northwest, Summer now lives in Northern Virginia with her husband of fifteen years, and their four children. A former public relations and political communications writer she left the corporate world to navigate the unappreciable waters of parenting as a stay-at-home mom. She had always been a story teller, and even from an early age would hand-write children's books that circulated amongst a dedicated following of 13 readers. This passion for writing, coupled with a desire to encourage other moms, and the attempt to keep her own sanity drew her into the world of motherhood blogging. She started Motherhood in Technicolor in 2014 after the birth of her fourth child in five years....a breeding plan she doesn't wildly recommend to most people. The inspiration for the title of her blog came from a Maya Angelou quote which referenced her mother causing a technicolor impression on her life. In addition to the daily exercise of capturing life lessons courtesy of her children, and observational insights from the world around her on the blog, she is a former Listen to Your Mother cast member, online publications author, and public speaker. She believes that motherhood is a shared experience, and that our children will ultimately teach us more than we will ever have the privilege to teach them.

WHERE DID MY SWEET LITTLE ONE GO?

TASH WARREN–JAMES

"Why are you such a massive pain?"
One mother asked her child
"You've been driving me insane,
"Since you became *so* vile."

"You used to be so loving;
"You used to be so sweet
"But love for mom means nothing,
"Now that you're a teen."

"You slam your door,
"Won't do as you're told,
"Ignore your chores,
"Act like you're *so* old!"

"Where did my sweet little one go?

"My cherub, my angel, *that* child?
"Not this moody thing with a ring through her nose,
"But the one who was gentle, and mild!"

***

This mother (as she told anyone who would listen),
Was reaching the end of her tether.
She'd cry with frustration – her eyes would glisten –
When she recounted her most recent endeavor.

For 'endeavor' was one way to put it.
Though 'begging' or 'pleading' might better explain
Her daily efforts, just *doing her bit*
To stop her daughter from being such a pain!

Her friends would nod, with weary recognition
When she spouted the latest event;
With teens of their own, they knew well the condition
Of teens spreading discontent.

The arguments, the bending of rules,
They knew just how bad it could be:
Battling at home, and battling at school;
It felt like battling was their new reality.

The mothers felt better, the more they shared,
They felt so much less alone.
They all loved their kids, they all *really* cared,
But sometimes it felt so good to moan!

***

The culprit of all this strife,
And the offender of all their woe;
The miscreant causing upset in their life,

Was something smaller ... than a toe!

Nestled in the brains of each of their teens,
Sat pituitary glands, just the size of a pea.
These glands were doing everything within their means
To encourage and advance puberty.[1]

This tiny yet powerful endocrine
Was behind all the recent surges -
The surges in emotions, in changes in skin,
New interests and unexplored urges.

This little gland is no stranger to hard work;
It proves size doesn't always matter.
It can bring on rapid growth spurts,
Affect our mood and even make us fatter!

***

Meanwhile, somewhere North East
- High up on a cloud -
A band of bearded men (or moustachioed at least)
Sat gathered in a round.

"That's what I call 'storm and stress',"[2]

---

1   The pituitary gland releases Follicle Stimulating Hormone (FSH) and Lu-
teinizing Hormone (LH), which trigger the body towards sexual maturity.

2   G. Stanley Hall, 1904. Hall was the first psychologist to put forward theo-
ries and methods for studying adolescents. He viewed the period between childhood
and adulthood as one of "*storm and stress*", likening adolescents to caged animals
who want their own freedom but are unable to always be free, creating within them a
sense of confusion and frustration.

The eldest one began.

"These teens are clearly in distress,

"As they grow from boy to man."

"These kids don't depend on their parents any more,"

Another bearded man proclaimed.

"At this stage they'll mainly want to explore",[3]

He succinctly and calmly explained.

"Explore their sexuality?"

Asked the third man, knitting his brow.

"I believe exploration of their *identity*,[4]

"Is the crucial struggle right now".

***

Now, as the men's discussion became somewhat fraught,

And as the mothers commiserated,

Let's turn to the teens, and give *them* some thought

... Perhaps their flaws have been over-stated?

"It's my *mom* who's not doing too well".

Said one fifteen-year-old, defiantly.

"She says I'm constantly trying to rebel

---

3   Sigmund Freud, 1915. In Freud's psychosexual theory of development, adolescents progress and mature through a 'Genital Stage' in puberty, looking outside the family to *explore* their sexuality and establish relationships.

4   Erik Erikson, 1968. Erikson's psychosocial theory of development considers the importance of society, proposing that adolescents go through a stage of 'crisis', whereby they seek to discover and establish their own *identities.*

"But I'm just carving out some autonomy!"

"My mom can't handle not knowing what to do,
"She thinks she's losing her role as caregiver.
"It's true I don't need her to brush my hair, or make me food
"But if she wasn't around, I'd miss her."

***

So.
It sounds like both parent and teen
Are in a process of flux.
They're both figuring out what their new roles mean
And until they do … this stage really sucks!

Tash Warren-James is a freelance writer, counsellor for children and young adults, singer-songwriter and (most recently) a mother. A bit of a nomad, she grew up in Europe, the Middle East and Asia, and now resides in beautiful Queensland, Australia.

PART II:
THE LAUGHS

Yes, there are some really challenging moments that come along with moving into the tween/teen years. But fear not. There is fun too. Embrace it all, including the awkward times.

"WHEN YOUR CHILDREN ARE TEENAGERS, IT'S IMPORTANT TO HAVE A DOG SO THAT SOMEONE IN THE HOUSE IS HAPPY TO SEE YOU."

—NORA EPHRON

THE BIRDS, THE BEES, AND THE FANCY MONEY SNATCHERS

ECHO ASPNES

Many parents dread having the conversation about the birds and the bees with their young tweens and teens. I was neither prepared nor expecting it when my son led us right into the conversation on sex and relationships. And boy did it go differently than I ever imagined.

"I know that I have to watch out for those **Fancy Money Snatchers**!"

That is not the type of thing you would expect to hear coming out of your pre-tween's mouth, yet I heard it come out of mine. I suppose I have heard weirder statements from my son, but this one had me intrigued.

My son has always been interested in nature documentaries. He has been watching them non-stop on Netflix. Normally, this would be a great thing, right? A child, watching educational programming. Well, this is a problem, because my son happens to be watching all of the nature documentaries on reproduction. Yup, that's right. He is learning about the "birds and the bees" from, well, the birds and the bees. I took this as a hint that it may be time to have a discussion with the boy.

"Hey buddy, let's have a little chat." I asked him to come join me at the table and proceed to fix a chocolate milk for him and a coffee for me. I fidgeted in my chair a little as he sat down.

He looked up at me with the swirly straw in his mouth and asked, "Am I in trouble?"

"No, you're not in trouble, but I want to talk to you about the documentaries that you've been watching."

"Oh, you mean the animal ones?"

"Yes, those. I noticed that they all have a specific theme."

He looks up at me, over the blue rims of his glasses and says, "You mean the continuation of the species?"

I tried to hide a smirk (although inside I'm certain I giggled) and said, "Yes, the continuation of the species. How much do you know about the continuation of your species?"

He stared at me blankly and then, slurped the last little bit of his chocolate milk down. Smacking his lips he said, "I know that males have the semen and women have the eggs. I also know that I'm not just going to give my semen to anyone. It needs to be the right female, with the right eggs. I think I'm like an Emperor Penguin, I only want to pick one and stick with that one for the rest of my life."

Did he really just say that? I asked myself in amazement. Despite my amazement, I nodded my head in agreement. He got all of this by watching animals and listening to David Attenborough?

"I'm happy to hear you say that, but the animal kingdom is a little more straight-forward than the human side of it," I say, as I prepare to tell him about liars, cheats and heartbreak.

"It's ok, mom," he says nonchalantly. "You don't have to worry. I know that I have to watch out for those *Fancy Money Snatchers!*"

"Fancy Money Snatchers?" I ask, stifling a chuckle.

"Yeah, you know, those girls that dress up 100% fancy, pretend to love you and then run away with all of your money! They are just Fancy Money Snatchers!" he shook his head. "I'm on the lookout for those."

"That's great, honey," I sputter as I finish choking on my coffee.

"So, is there anything else you want to talk to me about, mom?" he squirmed in his seat, eager to retreat back to his boy-cave and be illuminated by his EVER-impressive video games.

"No, buddy. As long as you stay away from those fancy money snatchers and save your semen for someone special, we are all good!"

"Ok, mom. I will. Can I go now?" he asked, already halfway out of his chair.

"Sure, kiddo! Have fun!'

So, you see, my son learned about the birds and the bees literally from the birds and the bees. And then he schooled me about those fancy money snatchers. While I know there will be much to learn about girls and heartache, I felt relieved that I didn't have to worry about him being taken advantage of for his money.

On a related note, thanks to the BBC's nature documentaries, my son believes that humans are pack animals. He has also decided that he would like to stay with his father and I forever, oh and raise his own children in our house too.

I weep for our future, but I can't tell you if they are tears of joy or tears of insanity.

Echo Aspnes pisses and moans about her kids. She loves, she cooks, she drinks coffee and laughs. Her motto is:If you aren't laughing in parenting, you are probably crying (or yelling). You can find her at <u>Facebook/themadmommy</u> *and @irkedmommy on* <u>Instagram</u> *and* <u>Twitter</u>

UNINTENTIONAL INSTA—SPY
LESLIE BLANCHARD

Sometimes, perfectly innocent parents are thrust into the helicopter-y role through absolutely no fault of their own. Parents who are not trying to monitor every move of their children and certainly aren't living vicariously through their children's adventures still wind up hovering anyway. Because their *child* made it happen.

We live in the day and age of social media, which is both a blessing and a curse. But the good side of it is we can now spy, I mean, participate, in the daily activities of our children. And boy is it entertaining.

I didn't intend to spy on my daughter, or to mortally embarrass her, but hey, it happened. And she did it to herself.

When our 18-year-old daughter was home from college recently she uploaded (or is it downloaded? I have absolutely no idea) her Instagram account onto my iPad.

I'm not 100% sure why she did this, but I can certainly speculate ...

It's not because her eyesight is failing, and she can't see her friends' pictures without the benefit of a larger screen. That would be *my issue,* as her 50-something-year-old mom. If I had to give a solid guess, it would be that her cell phone was dead, and my iPad was the only device that was charged at the moment. So, in the self-serving manner of every teenaged girl in America, she simply helped herself to my property.

After she performed this download/upload task, she cyber-socialized a bit and then drove herself back to The Mansion (they call it "The House") in the College Town where she currently resides at my expense. For anyone keeping track, that was on a Sunday afternoon.

Things were quiet for a few days. (For those of you not yet blessed with college students, these kiddos are super dedicated to their studies, and honoring your excruciating monetary investment for at least three days out of seven, so there's not a lot of traffic on the social highway Mondays-Wednesdays.) A few days later, I was unsuspectingly reading my book in my bed, minding my business, when all Hell broke loose.

"Notifications" start dinging away across the top of my screen, as though The Trans-Siberian Orchestra had set up right there inside my device to play my own personal lullaby. I fell asleep long before I had a chance to become annoyed, but it appears the dinging continued merrily on throughout the night.

The next morning I brewed my coffee and attempted to check my email. Upon opening my iPad I saw that my screen-saver had been blanketed overnight with a flurry of "LIKES" covering the iPad like the first snowfall of the season. At least 300 notifications! I could not imagine what I had done, who I had done it with, nor who all these people were who had liked it so much.

To be perfectly honest, I'm not sure I even had 300 people at my own wedding.

But, what did eventually dawn on me, as I took a few sips of coffee and arrived at full wakefulness, was that my daughter had to be buried somewhere under this avalanche of incessant social validation.

I waited for what I considered to be an extremely polite five hours before I called her. (We have radically different time schedules.) When I finally questioned her about it, *she* actually had the audacity to fuss at *me*.

"Whatever you do, Mom, do not hit the "LIKE" button on any of those pictures! In fact, you know what, don't even touch your iPad, I'll come home in a couple of days and delete the app!"

She actually told me *not to touch my iPad* until she could come home in a *couple* of days!

As if that weren't enough, she went on to further address my ignorance. "You have no idea how Instagram even works! I'm sure you don't remember, but you've actually embarrassed me once before. I know you don't understand technology, but that's MY account even though it's on YOUR iPad. So, it's the equivalent of me liking my own pictures! I'm really not trying to hurt your feelings, but it'd probably be best if you just steered clear of your iPad for now!"

A couple of things:

1. I truly appreciated that she wasn't trying to hurt my feelings.
2. I've only embarrassed her once before?

3. I use my iPad for work, so the mandate to "steer clear?" Probs not gonna happen.

Later that evening, around the same time, maybe a little later, the exact same thing happened. It seemed as though I was just as popular as I was the night before, with even more strangers dinging my praises!

Call it what you will: a flaw in my character, curiosity, helicopter parenting...I don't know, but, I could not seem to help myself. I closed out my book app and tapped on that camera-looking-thingy, devoting the rest of the evening to "blindly groping" my way around her Instagram account. I'm a firm believer in, "learning by doing," "trial and error," and, if all else fails, I'm not above a short YouTube tutorial.

Her Daddy and I had the most unapologetically entertaining weekend getting to know all of our daughter's friends intimately over Instagram. It was kind of like binge-watching a Netflix series starring Our Kid with her friends in supporting cast roles. Or like one of those college "Parent's Weekends," without all the unnecessary travel and costly hotel and restaurant charges.

And her chums had the cutest Instagram names! They reminded me of those old amusing CB monikers from the 1970s.

They were semi-incognito -- like "maddieboddie." I have a hunch that's my niece down in Louisiana. Hey Madeline -- Aunt Leslie loves you!

And "Imbringingsexyjack!" I'll just bet he is. He's bringing clever back is what he's doing.

And how about "thrillyjilly?" I bet that gal really can bring the thrill to a party. I'm wondering if her Daddy's seen that?

Speaking of CBs, I actually had a CB name when I was a kid -- "Brillo Pad!" They called them Handles for CB names too. Isn't that ironic? My handle was a reference to my frizzy hair. My parents thought of it. Evidentiary that parents in the 1970s weren't overly-consumed with the whole concept of self-esteem building...but I digress.

I was actually grateful for the barrage of notifications. My husband's demanding career in the restaurant business and the craziness of raising five children, means we rely heavily on each other to keep tabs on all of our children. (The main reason I'm so keen on updating my social media skills.)

So this morning, when he asked me if I'd heard anything from our middle daughter yet this weekend, I answered, "I haven't exactly heard from her, per se, but I can show "proof of life" with an adorable picture off of her Instagram account!"

I held up my iPad for his viewing pleasure. (When she's not annoyed with us, she really is such a little doll.) Intrigued and delighted, he reached out...

Don't.

Touch.

The.

Screen.

Oops, too late.

A red heart emoticon popped up right over the fluffy blonde head of "bythegracieofgod."

As you might imagine, she got an immediate notification on

her smart phone that the folks back home had not only just LIKED her picture on HER OWN INSTAGRAM account, But, actually just LOVED IT!

When she texted me that our social media faux pas was akin to telling the world that she loved herself, I responded that "surely her average follower had deduced that by now from the sheer volume of pictures she posted of herself on the daily..."

She's threatening to retaliate by deleting her Instagram account off my iPad as the first order of business when she gets home.

The real quandary now is that Daddy and I are so enamored with this voyeuristic notion of spying on our kids through Instagram, I'm going to be forced to revive my old CB HANDLE and start my own Insta...

"brillopad" didn't just LIKE your picture, she freaking LOVED it!

That's a big 10-4 Good Buddy!

Our kids turned out okay, and so will yours. Don't be afraid to monitor what they're doing on social media. It's much better to embarrass them than it is to wish you'd paid more attention.

On a beautiful afternoon at the end of January this year, Leslie's life was irrevocably changed when the Love of her Life, her husband of 33 years and father of their 5 children was killed in a motorcycle accident. Prior to that, Leslie's blog had been a mostly comical chronicle of marriage with a large family of teens and millennials. Now she shares her daily experiences as she comes to terms with her profound sadness and shock, coupled with an

effort to ever-capture even the lighter side of the most unimagin-
ably painful challenges life can throw one's way. She has been
featured in Your Teen Magazine, and on websites such as Blunt
Moms, Scary Mommy, BonBon Break, Lose The Cape, Today's
Parent, BlogHer, and Faithit. She has been interviewed on NPR
and is also proud to be liberally splashed about The Huffing-
ton Post in the United States, France, Spain, Japan, Quebec and
Germany. Get more from Leslie at: http://agingersnapped.com

VASELINE®
HEATHER LEROSS

Don't let the title of this essay weird you out. I'm not going to share any stories that would leave you disturbed and mortify my son. I'll just tell you that Vaseline was one of many unexpected adventures in adolescence I was unprepared to face as the mother of boys.

I didn't know what to expect from motherhood when I was pregnant the first time. I knew what I wanted; lots of cuddles, laughs, Barbie dolls, pink rooms, manicures and pedicures with my mini-me. I wanted the joy of introducing my daughter to make-up, my love of books, spa days, and everything else girly. Realistic? Not really since my first-born daughter came out a boy. I remember being shocked in the ultrasound when the tech said my daughter had a penis.

"I think you're mistaken. Girls have vaginas," I lamely replied having decided on the table to "school" the ultrasound technician. Ultimately, she won this battle.

I claim early onset Mommy-brain or denial, or just plain idiocy. Whatever it was, to say I was in disbelief is an understatement. This meant I had to rush home, delete all the saved links (this was pre-Pinterest days) I had to the girl's room décor

I'd bookmarked, find the receipt for the pink stuffed bear and dress I'd already bought, and start searching out "boy stuff," which is actually what I typed into the search box that day. Boy stuff.

I was clueless about "boy stuff" in all ways. I was thrilled to be having a healthy baby, and once I found that there were some cute boy stuffs out there, I figured I could manage this whole boy-mom ride I was on. We could still cuddle, I could still show him the joys of escaping into a book, and maybe he'd like some blue toenails (which did in fact happen). Whew!

When pregnant again, this time with my daughter, I was more relaxed. I'd managed five years of being a boy-mom and had done a relatively decent job (he was still alive), so I knew motherhood was do-able. I was really looking forward to some mommy-daughter time while my son played video games with his dad.

While I'd love to say having my second child was everything I had imagined, having another daughter with a penis put a crimp in my plans for mommy-daughter bonding. Good thing I'd smartly saved all the clothes and toys from my first son, so my second boy had lots of blues, greens, yellows, cars and dinosaurs to adorn his masculine baby body and stimulate his boy brain.

I adjusted to all boy-mom life and honestly, I thoroughly enjoyed being the only princess in the house. Nothing melted my heart more than hearing my boys tell me they loved me and that I was beautiful, something my youngest would say with a smile, his dimpled cheeks chubby and irresistible to kisses.

That is, until we hit the tweens, followed rapidly by the teen years.

Before I knew what hit me I was awash in acne, smells emanating from my oldest son's room that made me wonder if he was harboring dead bodies that had been marinated in onions (what's with the onion smell??), and girls. Girls. I was now faced with questions like, "Why do girls care so much about how they look? Why do girls act so weird around guys? Why did (insert girl name here) get so mad when I told her I liked (insert DIFFERENT girls name)?"

Ummm, because they're girls and we like to feel like we're the most liked (even if we don't like you back), and we act weird because we're insecure mostly, and OHMYGODIDONTKNOW!! It was like I became the guru of all things female and even though I am female, I don't even know why I do the things I do sometimes. Trying to explain ALL GIRLS to my son was taxing. Plus, it made me examine why I did/do the things I do and ugh, I didn't always like what I discovered. My advice? I got nothing y'all. Wing it?

Turns out, girls were the easy part. It was the Vaseline that really caught me off guard. I'd long ago bought the Costco sized jar of Vaseline for my son's dry skin, chapped lips, and whatever hell else we use 6lbs of Vaseline for. I'd left it in his room since he used it most. Once teen years hit, I discovered the jar was empty. His lips weren't chapped much anymore, and I was puzzled as to what how he could go through that much Vaseline. Have you figured it out yet?? It took me a bit but it all clicked into place when I was talking my ex who told me he found a small jar of Vaseline in my son's pillowcase. Bingo. I'm a cool mom though so I made sure this year his stocking was stuffed with a Costco sized jar of Vaseline. Thankfully, my son has a good sense of humor, knows I know about this "stash," and laughed and thanked me.

My advice: set up a recurring delivery for Vaseline with Amazon. You'll even get a discount for recurring shipments!

I have a few more pointers for moms of boys approaching adolescence.

Hygiene. Basically, with teen boys, there is none. Showers I think are just a nice 30-minutes-alone-and-naked time to do as they please, but *never* with soap or shampoo. Just expenditure of the household supply of hot water, until you wonder if they've drowned.

My advice: Always take your shower/bath FIRST.

Poop. Sorry to get gross (seriously, raising teen boys is a whole lotta gross, so get used to it), but what is up with the hour-long trips to the bathroom? I swear one boy has pooped for, and I am NOT kidding, two hours. Two hours he was in the bathroom! I know they take their devices with them these days so it's not all pooping but ummm, GROSS! They're locked in a tiny room with the smell of their crap all around them. These kids have their own rooms. Why not dump and run back to the safeness of their boy-caves? Why spend so much time in stink? I think boys' noses are truly broken.

My advice: None. Just let them enjoy their marathon craps. And stock up on air freshener.

Food. Holy shit where do they put all of the food? I don't seem to be able to buy enough some weeks to keep my boys alive. Thankfully, it's not constant eating yet because my oldest has an aversion to movement (he's happiest on the couch, which

I'm not proud of but hey, there's bugs outside) which means he saves calories. But my youngest is active and hungry. Hungry like I'm sure he has no stomach, just an open cavity inside that needs to be filled with food. But some days, there aren't enough boxes of cereal, fruit and Hot Pockets. Don't judge, I'm trying here. They do eat kale chips, broccoli and spinach salad, and chips to keep them fueled. My nightmares now revolve around waking up to find the pantry is empty and not being able to get out to the store because my kids got so hungry they turned into Zombies and are now hunting in the neighborhood (I understand this is not how Zombies are actually created, but dreams don't always make sense y'all). That one might have been after a few glasses of wine but still, frightening!

My advice: Buy food. Buy ALL the food.

Friendships. I don't get boy friendships. I thought teen girls were tough on one another. Boys seem to be just as ruthless and cruel at times. I thought maybe it was just the group of boys my oldest son hangs out with, but in talking with my ex and my current husband, this is pretty normal. My son has been called every hurtful name in the book, been shunned, which these days means he was kicked out of the group video game they were playing online, and punched (in the arm but still, ouch). He rolls with it and says he's fine with it because he knows this is just how boys are. What happened to whispering behind your friend's back, spreading rumors about Becky being "easy," and laughing when Lily wore skinny jeans which are now "soooo, 1989?" Oh right, it's not 1989, and once again IDONTKNOWWHATSUPWITHKIDS!

My advice: Keep the doors of communication as open as you can. This is sometimes akin to telling you to climb a mountain in high heels while running, but I do know our kids hear us. Even when we think they don't. Keep repeating that you're there for them, keep reminding them they're loved and safe with you. It does sink in.

Finally, the joy. There is so much joy in seeing the amazing men my sons are becoming; it is astounding that I created them. They make me laugh, they challenge me to look at things from a different perspective, and their empathy for others knows no bounds. I'm grateful they still come to me with questions, concerns, for comfort, and my youngest thanks me after every meal I make for him, gives me a hug, and tells me he loves me.

In summary:

Teenage boys. They smell. They use up all the water and eat all the food. They have questions I can't answer, hurts I can't heal, dreams I can't always fulfill. They put kindness into the world, they make me scream in frustration at times, and other times weep with gratitude. I'm proud of who they are, I will worry about them until I am no longer with them, and I love them more than they know.

Heather LeRoss is an imperfect human trying to raise perfect humans. As the mom of 2 boys of her own and a step-son, she lives in the gross world of boys who argue about using soap in the shower and ensure the dog always has fun stuff to lick in the bathroom. Author of the book, Just Tell Me I'm Pretty: Musings on a Messy Life, she writes to connect women who feel alone, who are missing a village of support. She writes for the mother of a special needs child who's not sure how she is going to manage one more melt-down, one more parent-teacher conference, or one more day. She writes for the women who pee their pants when they sneeze, cry during commercials for diapers, and who still want to sometimes hear, "You're pretty."

Follow the funny on FB at
https://www.facebook.com/tipsytiaras
Read the latest and greatest on her blog at
http://www.tipsytiaras.com
See her embarrassing photos on Instagram at
http://www.instagram.com/tipsytiaras

THE HAIR
JENNIFER ROSEN HEINZ

I still read aloud to my 11-year-old son. I know lots of people don't still read to their kids when they hit the tween years, but both of my kids have always loved our reading time. When my son was just a baby (and yes, I do mean *baby*) he would demand, cry, crab, grouse, and grow quite unhappy if I was not reading to him.

I stayed home with him full time when he was little, and by the age of 1 1/2 he had me reading to him almost nonstop, all day long. Like *seven hours long*. Reading to him was, in a sense, a full-time job. This may sound extreme (it was) or like an exaggeration (it's not). He loved books. and had a crazy, long attention span. It was likely because he was born with a congenital cataract in his left eye, which seriously impacted his vision. He wanted me, his person, close. He wanted to look at things that were also close. His love of reading was as much a product of his physical limitations as it was due to his love of illustrations and stories.

Fast forward to the age of 11, he was entering the tween domain. The push-pull of wanting to be nurtured and wanting to have separation from me had already started. He wasn't always certain he wanted to cuddle at night. But reading—that was a non-negotiable. Reading had to happen.

As he matured, of course our choice in reading material changed as well. Often, I can get away with reading things to him that might be more difficult than what he would choose because I can be his guide. I provide historical perspective. Color commentary. I define words or concepts that might be difficult. I help him appreciate foreshadowing and character development, and I ask him his opinions.

So one night, there we are. He was showered and in bed, I was nestled alongside him reading. I noticed that he kept making some repetitive movement, and it was getting annoying because even the slight movement made the hand I held the book with wiggle, and that annoyed me.

"What are you doing? Stop doing it!" I said, without looking up from the book.

"I'm just playing with my armpit," he said.

"Why are you playing with your armpit?" I said. "Is there something wrong with it?"

"Well, sort of," he replied.

"What?" I asked, a bit incredulous. "How can you not know if there is something wrong?"

"Well...," he said haltingly, "I am playing with a hair."

"A hair?" I asked.

"A hair," he repeated.

"Don't you mean *hairs*?" I asked. While I suspected at some point he would start to grow hair under his arms, I was a little surprised that it would start at 11. And that it would only be ... *one*? "Are you sure?" I asked.

"Yep. It's *one long* hair," he replied.

"Let me see that," I said, half-thinking that he was not perceiving his situation correctly. I mean, how could he? He couldn't really *see* his armpit in its totality to assess the situation.

He pulled at his t-shirt sleeve and lifted his arm to reveal his pale armpit. I moved in closer to survey the area.

Lo and behold, there it was. *The hair.*

A flaxen lightening bolt. The *first* hair.

It was not just *there*, it was charged by some kind of static electricity. Like one of those car dealership blow-up windsock people who buck around to grab attention of traffic.

"Oh my god!" I shouted, without an iota of self-control, "It's A HAIR! ONE HAIR! ONE LONE HAIR!" and we both started whooping with laughter. Tears streamed down our faces. I laughed so hard and in such paroxysm that I got a Charley horse in my foot. My face hurt.

BANG BANG BANG my seven-year-old daughter was knocking on the wall, "I'm trying to sleep in here!" she yelled, somewhat muffled.

"I know! I'm sorry!" I yelled, as we whooped and hooted anew.

After a solid three minutes, I asked him if I could see it again to take a closer look. He obliged.

He was very proud of his one hair. It had character. He had recently transformed almost instantly from a somewhat shy, reticent child, to a jokester. He purposefully was pushing his boundaries, trying to figure out how to participate in the more adult world of political humor, expanding on his love of puns and wordplay.

"I am proud of my hair," he admitted. "I will call him Dr.

Phil."

"Dr PHIL?! How do you even KNOW who Dr. Phil is?!"

"Well," he said, "Our health teacher showed us some special that Dr. Phil did about eating disorders. There is something about him that is kind of funny, so I was walking around after class trying to do his voice for my friends."

"OK, Dr. Phil it is, then. Is Dr. Phil bothering you at all? Why are you messing with him?"

"Dr. Phil IS bothering me," he admitted. "Mom," he asked, "could you please give him a trim? At least make him a little shorter. You know, until he has more company."

So, I left the room, collected a tiny pair of nail scissors, and carefully trimmed Dr. Phil to a respectable 1/2-inch length. As I held Dr. Phil between my fingers, we both inspected him in the light.

"You should be very proud of Phil," I said. "Your body grew him all by itself. Shall we save him? You know, like we saved your baby teeth?"

His face lit up, "That would be awesome!"

I retrieved a Ziploc baggie, which I labelled neatly with permanent marker "RIP PHIL." I inserted the golden hair, closed it up and said, "Now put it under your pillow tonight just in case there's a hair fairy!"

We laughed again, and instead of putting it under his pillow, we put it on his bedside table while we finished our chapter in the book, before marking our place for the next night, putting the book aside, and turning off the lamp.

I never thought that I would have a son (somehow, to me, all babies were girls by default). When I had a son, I knew that

I had to, in whatever way I could, help him to keep his body safe and allow it to grow and develop. While some parents are (understandably) reticent about the bursting forth of puberty, somehow, through grace, I was able to experience it with my son with a sense of humor and wonder. Celebrate it, even.

Since that night when Dr. Phil burst onto the scene, we have had many talks about bodies and development and love and relationships and friends. They almost always happen at night. After the reading is done, and the light goes out. There's something about that darkness that caters to conversations. I'm so thankful he talks with me about his friendships, his goals, his fears, worries, and now, about a girl he likes.

I have to think that this is all related. The small things *are* the big things, especially when the big things (love, relationship, changes, bodies) are awkward. That saying, "Don't sweat the small stuff, and it's all small stuff" is, in a sense, correct. The small stuff is putting in the time. The small stuff is reading. The small stuff is asking his opinion and listening to it. The small stuff is a small, but mighty, armpit hair, who just happens to be called Dr. Phil.

Jennifer Rosen Heinz has been accused of having the maturity of a nine-year-old boy because of her love of poop and fart jokes. She lives in Madison, Wisconsin and works for the parenting web site Scary Mommy. She is a recovering MFA and award-winning poet and blogger. Follow her at: http://the-thinking-mom.blogspot.com

PUBERTY: JUST AROUND THE CORNER
CHRISTINA SURRETSKY

I know what you're thinking. You've read the title of this article and you're thinking, "Gosh, I have a (insert age of child here). I don't have to worry about this for a LONG time." Really? Well, blink. Now blink again. One more time. Okay . . . it's here.

I know you think it's a long way off, but my oldest was five years old when he first asked where babies came from. FIVE. He was in Kindergarten. He was still picking his nose and occasionally asking me to wipe his butt. But he wanted to know WHERE BABIES CAME FROM.

I thought the sex talk was going to be the most awkward conversation I ever had with my child. It was not. Oh, don't get me wrong, it was uncomfortable, but then one day at the age of 10 my son came home and said, "Mom, in a few weeks we're going to see a video about puberty at school. It's called, 'Puberty: Just Around the Corner.' It has a dancing penis in it. A sixth grader told me so." And, thus began the long, uncomfortable, never-ending conversation about puberty. A conversation that has continued, randomly, over the course of the last several years and one that feels like it will not end until my child's entire body is covered in hair and he has fathered at least three children.

The sex talk was uncomfortable, but at least it was cut and dry. Tab A goes into slot B. In nine months, pull baby out of Slot B. And he was young enough not to have a lot of starting knowledge so there weren't *that* many extraneous questions. However, fast-forward five years and it's a whole, new world. A world filled with way too many inappropriate songs, video games, TV shows, and YouTube. To completely filter it all would require living without electricity. (And even then, I'm pretty sure he'd find an old National Geographic magazine somewhere.) This information base led to a thirst for knowledge that I did not anticipate.

"So, Mom, what happens to your body during puberty?"

"Don't you want to wait for the video? I mean, they have graphics. And a dancing penis."

"No, I want a preview."

If I thought the video was going to get me off the hook, I was wrong. My eldest son is not afraid to ask the tough questions, like the Barbara Walters of his generation.

"So. What happens?"

"Um, well, your body will go through . . . changes."

"Like what? Be specific."

"Um, well, your voice is going to get deeper."

I decided to start with the easy stuff. No use going right into a discussion about genitalia when I knew there was the possibility of redirecting him with exactly how deep and manly his voice might sound in a few years.

"What else?"

"Uh . . . you're going to grow hair on your body."

"Where?"

"Um. Everywhere."

Despite the fact that my husband is not a hairy man, my child, both children in fact, have already exhibited a predisposition to inherit their mother's hairy, Italian genes. In fact, I think I started to see the faintest outline of five o'clock shadow starting on my boys at around the age of seven.

"What else?"

"And . . . uh . . . you'll get more muscular and taller."

By this point, I was pretty sure he could sense my fear, knowing that I was running out of vague, innocuous things to say. Knowing we were headed into clinical territory.

"And. What. Else."

What followed was a fairly uncomfortable series of statements related to private parts and what happens to those private parts during puberty. It wasn't fun. But my son sucked up the knowledge like a dry sponge. And, I thought, "Great! Well, at least THIS is over with."

And then they showed the video.

This video should have made my life easier. I mean, the school nurse did all the heavy lifting, right? She's the one who had the puberty talk with a classroom full of boys. (An ENTIRE classroom! As far as I'm concerned, one is too many for this talk.) She's the one who had to talk about the dancing penis with a straight face. She's the one who fielded the hard questions.

But it did not.

"Can your balls really turn blue during puberty?"

"Do you know what nocturnal emissions are? Don't be

fooled. It has nothing to do with the environment."

"Do girls masturbate?"

No matter what question I answered, it didn't satisfy my child. He wanted more.

"Mom, you know the girls had to watch a video about puberty, too. And you know how we got deodorant and mouthwash? Well, they got pamphlets."

"Pamphlets? You got a pamphlet, too."

"No, I didn't."

"Yes, you did. A pamphlet is that little paper booklet of information you got telling you about puberty."

"Oh! Yeah! I mixed it up. They got tampons! What's a tampon?"

Sensing my unease with the direction of the conversation, tampon became the word of the day for my children. "Tampon!" they would shout, randomly, in my direction. Until I could take it no more.

"The next person to utter the word 'tampon' will lose all of their electronics for the day!" I shouted.

Then my son muttered something under his breath.

"What did you say?" The unspoken threat was evident in my tone.

"Tan mom. I just said, 'tan mom' is all. Tan mom! Tan mom!"

So, it continues. The ongoing curiosity and the continuous questions. But no matter how uncomfortable or explicit the question, I will always answer every one, because just by nature of the fact that he's willing to ask it means I must be doing something right. And, let's face it I'm terrified of what he might find if he tried to answer it himself with Google.

"Mom! Come here! I think I have a hair on my chest!"

"It's just an eyelash."

"What about under my arms?"

"That's fuzz from your shirt."

"Oh well. Hey, Mom? Do you think puberty will be kind to me? You know, it's not kind to some people."

"I think puberty will be very kind to you."

Unfortunately, I don't think it will be very kind to me.

Christina Surretsky did not actually want to be a writer when she grew up. She wanted to be Wonder Woman, Princess Leia, or one of Charlie's Angels. After the realization that none of these would pan out, she decided to pursue a career in business, getting her undergraduate degree in Marketing from St. John's University and her MBA from New York University. After a career in advertising (which she's sad to say is nothing like "Bewitched" or "Melrose Place") and then a gig as a mother (a field in which she currently still dabbles), she eventually heard the siren's call of the pen (or, really, the computer) and began her career as a writer. Her first novel, "Divine Bloodlines," a funny, contemporary, teenage-angst filled entry to the YA paranormal romance genre was published in 2014, and she is currently working on the sequel. She lives in New Jersey with her husband and her two sons, one of whom read her book and proclaimed it "the best book I've ever read and I'm not just saying that because you're my mom."

PART 3

VALUES, TOUGH SUBJECTS, AND DIFFICULT DECISIONS

This section is our perspective on teaching our tweens and teens about values and how to be good humans, how we grow relationships, and making difficult decisions when it comes to parenting a teen. And naturally, we cover the struggles we face in the process.

"MOTHER NATURE IS PROVIDENTIAL. SHE GIVES US TWELVE YEARS OF DEVELOPING A LOVE FOR OUR CHILDREN BEFORE SHE TURNS THEM INTO TEENAGERS."

—WILLIAM GALVIN

A FAMILY THAT PLAYS TOGETHER
KATHERINE MIKKELSON

One Saturday evening a few years ago, I announced to my boys we were going apple picking the next day.

"Awww, Mom, do we have to?" asked my younger son, 14 at the time, as if I just told him we were required to scrub latrines for an entire day instead of taking a beautiful drive to southern Wisconsin.

"It's going to be a nice day and we don't have anything else going on," I replied. Rare was there a Sunday in fall with no soccer games, no swim meets, no band competitions.

"But Mom, I'll miss my games!" said my older son, 17 at the time and already panicking to miss his regularly scheduled football viewing.

"We'll go early. We'll even skip church. You'll be back in time for the games. You won't miss a minute," I said.

More moans, frowns, and general grumbling.

"They have apple cinnamon milkshakes! And cider donuts!" I enthused.

My husband had observed this exchange thus far without uttering a word. Now he piped up. "We're going. FFF."

That was it. End of conversation. Forced Family Fun—a

phrase my husband and I coined a while back—had been declared, and my kids knew further argument was fruitless (yup, pun intended).

It's a well-known fact teenagers don't want to hang out with their parents. I didn't want to hang out with mine, our parents didn't want to hang out with theirs and I'm pretty sure Cain and Abel didn't want a thing to do with Adam and Eve. Parents are dorky/stupid/uncool/weird/boring — pick your favorite adjective. But if FFF is not invoked from time to time, we would rarely, if ever, see our teenage sons. They'd rather be doing other, more important things, like hanging out with their friends, tethered to their devices, keeping real interaction to a minimum.

With teens though, for FFF to be effective, certain rules must be followed to ensure maximum pleasure for all concerned parties.

No. 1: FFF must involve food or the promise of being fed. Nothing is more excruciating than a teenager who complains and whines that he is "so hungry he could literally eat a cow." If you want to take your kids to a baseball game when they would rather stay home and play MLB on PlayStation, tell them they can get a hot dog, nachos, ice cream served in the little batting helmet and a slice of pizza. Yes, you will have to take out a home equity line of credit to finance this, but on the plus side, the constant chewing and swallowing is pretty effective in preventing them from asking every half hour about when you can leave.

No. 2: FFF must involve physical activity or the observ-

ing of someone else engaged in physical activity. When we traveled to Canada several summers ago, I wanted to rent bikes and cycle around Stanley Park, Vancouver's equivalent of Central Park. This was met with a lukewarm response until I mentioned it would take no longer than an hour and that I would buy everyone ice cream cones at Prospect Point (see rule 1 above and rule 3 below).

No. 3: FFF must be short. While several hours can be tolerated, shorter stints are better. The apple picking literally took half an hour, with a quick 30-minute drive each way. The church picnic is two hours, tops, even with the Baggo tournament. Family parties should last only as long as it takes to get the burgers off the barbeque and a quick game of whiffle ball.

Despite all the protests, FFF is sure to bring your family together. Nothing brings a satisfied smile to a parent's face quicker than a teen that grouses but then ends up having fun.

I was on the other end of FFF several winters ago in Florida when my mom insisted we drive to the county dump to bird watch. We all exchanged dubious glances with each other. The dump? Really?

"Come on, it'll be fun. It's not far and we won't stay long. And I'll treat you to lunch afterward," she promised.

We all protested but piled into the van for the short drive. The dump actually had a bird-watching guide that they handed out to visitors and sure enough, as we hiked around, we saw bald eagles, turkey vultures, and Sandhill cranes, not to mention scores of feral pigs.

"That was really fun," said Zack, as he sat munching his

sub sandwich 30 minutes later.

"Yeah," said AJ. "Those piglets were so cute."

My mom smiled. I knew I learned FFF from somewhere.

Katherine Mikkelson is a recovering attorney turned writer. She writes a food blog called StateEats (http://stateeats.com) and her work has appeared in Adoptive Families Magazine and the Chicago Tribune. An essay, "The Things You Do For Love" appeared in the anthology, Here In the Middle: Stories of Love, Loss, and Connection from the Ones Sandwiched in Between (220 Publishing, 2016). She lives in the Chicago area with her husband Tom and is the mother of two boys.

THIS MOM IS NOT YET RATED

DANIELLE SILVERSTEIN

When I was four years old, my mom took me to my first movie. I still remember the excitement of having the huge screen in front of me, sitting next to my mom, older sister, and brother, with my popcorn and soda. I waited with anticipation for the movie to start, and before I knew it Dolly Parton appeared, larger than life in The Best Little Whore House in Texas.

Ok, so it was a questionable choice of a movie for a toddler. By today's standards, she probably would have been all over social media with hashtags like #LittlestShameHouse or something ridiculous. Luckily, in 1982 social media did not exist, and there were also fewer movie choices to which you could take your kids. But if I'm completely honest, I have no recollection of being affected by the sex scenes in that movie. I don't know if my mom covered my eyes or took me to the bathroom during those parts. I do, however, have a deep, emotional memory of how much I loved watching the dancing, and hearing Dolly sing "I Will Always Love You." That experience remains one of my favorites and that movie will always carry a special place in my heart.

I won't pretend that was a one-time liberal movie or TV choice allowed by my mother. There were very few rules about what my siblings and I could watch. My childhood was filled with Flash-dance episodes and I'm certain I didn't even really understand what Jennifer Beals› job was; I just knew I desperately wanted an off-the-shoulder sweatshirt. I think it's worth noting: I never left to join a brothel, and to this day I have a total appreciation that stripping is hard work and people do it because it pays damn well. Overall, I feel good about the way I turned out, and I love my mom for not overly sheltering me and for trusting that, with her help and openness, I could handle some more mature scenarios.

Fast forward 30 years and it's my turn to decide what is and is not appropriate for my kids to watch, listen to, and play. How do I balance this new world of easy access to media satu-rated with sex, drugs, and violence with my own beliefs, like my mom's, to want my kids to partake in the magic and won-ders of amazing storylines and entertainment? I want them to delve into plots that are controversial enough that they spark a dozen deep questions to which I am able to help them explore the answers.

My 11-year-old daughter has a fascination and obsession with books, movies, and TV shows. I am somewhat blessed that she is very aware and confident of the person she wants to be. The decision to allow her to have a very loose range of what to watch was sort of easy, and we have had some amazing bond-ing days binge-watching movies with our favorite actors like Tina Fey, Amy Poehler, and Melissa McCarthy. She can even speak to adults about topics such as Maggie Smith's versatile acting style and knows the importance Meryl Streep has had on women's place in the film industry. She is, in some ways, a pop culture savant. I am both insanely impressed and somewhat concerned about this. There is little place in society to become a success because of one's extensive knowledge of the most profound coming-of-age movies of the 1990's, or the top 10 best sitcoms of all time. There are also plenty of times I cut her off from watching four consecutive hours of a show and force her to do something more "productive."

In a nutshell, I'm still figuring it all out. Every sleepover my kids have with their friends at our house has to be prefaced with, "Remember, not all kids are allowed to watch Pitch Perfect or Billy Madison, and I don't need to get a phone call from a mom tomorrow." There are plenty of times when I'll start watching a movie with my kids and realize I've forgotten several scenes that are in it and turn it off because it is too inappropriate even by my standards. But by staying true to my desire for my kids to experience the magic of real comedy, drama, and classics that I once was trusted to, regardless of some curse words and make out scenes (they cover their eyes anyway), some very positive things have occurred.

Because I have these open conversations with my kids about our beliefs on topics, they have an understanding for why some things happen that aren't appropriate for them to repeat or do. My nine-year-old son has a genuine understanding of why (in my opinion) the use of guns in some war movies are ok and even necessary, while guns in violent games like Call of Duty are unnecessary. He also understands that when Green

Day, his favorite band, curses, it's because they are passionate about a political message; a message we have spoken about numerous times and he understands well.

I believe the benefits of allowing these elements in their lives far outweighs the negatives. I never choose to let them watch a movie based solely on its rating, but rather on content. Some PG-13 movies have messages I don't want shared, and some R-rated movies have a crucial lesson that completely overshadows one or two questionable scenes. Watching certain films and shows and listening to some "explicit" albums has undoubtedly helped instill a deep-rooted sense of acceptance and admiration for people of all different races, sexual orientations, and religions. To me, this is invaluable.

For now, I'm going to keep trusting my kids to experience these same situations until they seem negatively affected by it. I'm also going to constantly talk to them about what they are seeing and hearing and use it as an opportunity to open a dialogue that we may not otherwise have. I'm hopeful that one day they will appreciate the fact that I gave them the opportunity to experience amazing cinema and it helped to shape them into individuals who base his or her decisions on what feels right, and not solely by what they've seen on a TV screen.

Whether or not my daughter winds up in the film or TV industry and becomes a famous screenwriter like she dreams of doing, I think being exposed to so many different genres and medium have helped put her and my boys on the path to become socially aware, perceptive, and accepting human beings. For now, that's enough for me to see that I've made the right decision for my kids to show them different points of view, thoughts, and practices with the intent of opening their minds and hearts to topics they would not otherwise been introduced.

Danielle Silverstein is a SAHM of three kids and two rescue dogs in New Jersey. Her blog, Where The Eff Is My Handbook, is meant to help women get through this crazy journey of motherhood with lots of humor and support. When she's not blogging and momming, Danielle loves to run, try new restaurants and travel. Look for the hilarious and heartfelt podcast she and her husband will be publishing very soon, called Marriage and Martinis. In the meantime, find her at Facebook.com/wheretheeffismyhandbook and on instagram at @wheretheeffismyhandbook.

HOW TO RAISE A FEMINIST IN 3 EASY STEPS

SHANTI BRIEN

Just the other day, as my 16-year-old daughter Lilli washed the dishes from her vegan-churro-making-explosion that she called an assignment for Spanish class, she said to me, "I don't know how anyone could do this all day. Being a stay-at-home mom would suck."

"No shit," I thought.

In the moment, I managed to say that parenting is hard work and a lot of satisfaction comes from raising kids. Some people think it's the most important job they can do. She responded with a teenage "hmpf" and continued scraping the flour and water mixture that had turned to cement on the counter.

I didn't tell Lilli that I am not one of those "fully-satisfied" mothers. In fact, I hate being a mother. I love my kids, of course, but I hate the expectations of motherhood: I should love babies, self-sacrifice, play dates and preparing organic meals with a smile. I should "do what's best for my kids" even when that includes a stagnant career, feelings of purposelessness and preoccupations with the library fair, the inauthentic accents of the

Spanish teachers and $6000 SAT tutors. I still find it tedious to attend school concerts with bad music. I loathe driving the soccer carpool.

On the other hand, I cherish the feelings of accomplishment and freedom I get from being an attorney, a professor, and a business owner. At one point when my kids were three and 18 months, I found it practically orgasmic to shower, put on a suit, and commute to the city for a rare court appearance.

I want to raise girls who value both their career AND the joys of motherhood, despite the moments that I don't love.

But how do I explain this to my daughter who is on the verge of womanhood? How do I explain these complicated choices to a young woman who already detests the idea of washing dishes all day? And how do I do it in a way that she doesn't feel resentment from me over the choices I made? How do I ensure she knows I adore her and she's worth the near endless friend/boyfriend/Instagram dramas?

How does a feminist mom who values both her career and raising her children bring up feminist kids, who also see the value of following their dreams while not making them feel like they ruined my dreams?

The reality is, the kids have caused career setbacks. And let's be honest; not all moments of raising kids can feel rewarding. Family life can be disgusting. Just tonight, Lilli asked her dad if she could pop a zit on his nose at the dinner table. Ceci threatened to walk away and the rest of us agreed. After dinner, Ceci picked at her callused big toe while sitting on the kitchen counter and I found yet another live cricket in my bathroom. It had escaped Zach's bearded dragon's enclosure. This was just one night! Despite the frustrating moments, it's worth it.

I think I have found a way I to teach my kids that a mom can love her kids, raise successful and caring people, and simultaneously remain a successful professional and impactful community member.

I have employed three basic strategies:

1. Bribery

Every summer, we "reward" our kids if they read a book a week. We don't normally employ this parenting tactic, but it's just enough motivation to get them a summer full of mind expansion. Last summer we counted Chimamanda Ngozi Adichie's book *We All Should Be Feminists*. It's a short, easy read with a clear message. Our daughters got to credit the book for an entire week. I got them to listen to an important young and international voice. We've also tackled *Lean In* by Sheryl Sandberg and we welcome anything by June Jordan or Naomi Wolf.

The Frida Kahlo exhibit? I'll pay for it. An internship at Girls, Inc? We'll let you out of your obligation to make money this summer. Miss school to protest the lead misogynist of the free world? Of course.

2. Enrolling Dad

This was not exactly difficult. My husband has always been a feminist. Still, as a former NFL player, for most of his adulthood he would have avoided that label. Since having two daughters, his level of commitment to the equality of the sexes had grown exponentially. He's practically demanding our daughters keep their last name if they get married. When Lilli had a boyfriend, Doug required him to proclaim his dedication. "I'm a feminist," Doug said to him at dinner one night, "You are too, right?"

3. Modeling

This is a basic parenting tool recommended by all the parenting experts. Model the behavior that you are teaching. At family dinners I talk about my gratitude for my work, how I love helping and teaching people. Doug and I model sharing housework, childcare, carpools (an increasingly daunting task) and extended "tuck ins" and other night-time rituals for our younger son. I campaigned for Hillary, including a trip to Nevada for poll-monitoring.

I also expose my kids to other models. Their doctor and dentist are both women-of-color. Luckily, California has had two female Senators for as long as my kids have been alive. Both daughters have had powerful and assertive female coaches.

It's a running family joke that Doug cannot do laundry. I've made it clear that if my daughters choose to marry someone, they will not only discuss and agree about children, child-care, household jobs and careers, but they will also consider his/her mother and the role she played in her family. If she modeled exclusive rights to all things domestic, it's a no-go.

In the end, praying that my kitchen would survive the churning churro chaos, I felt proud of Lilli for her drive to do more than cook and clean. She had previously expressed budding feminism. She played on her high school football team her Freshman year--the only girl on the team. She retired after one year because it just "wasn't fun." She never fit into the "brotherhood" and it was lonely blazing a trail. But she joined the feminist club at school, considers herself part of Pantsuit Nation, and clearly understands the dissatisfaction of folding laundry and scrubbing toilets.

I've never told my kids about my disdain for housework and my frustrations with the concept of motherhood with all its expectations, traps, and goriness. There are some things they don't need to know, nor would they truly be able to understand. I have faith that the lessons I impart on my children, plus what they learn on their own, will be enough. Seems like Lilli is learning it on her own, one vegan and culturally-diverse mess at a time.

Shanti Brien is a recovering-NFL wife and mother of three. As an attorney she formerly represented convicted criminals and now, through her company Fogbreak Justice, teaches criminal justice professionals and other public servants complex skills like increasing fairness, engaging residents and creating inclusion. As a writer, Shanti blogs on Medium about mothering, growing up Oakie and Indian, and her life with criminals and potential criminals. She also writes about teaching and lawyering for Ms. JD.

WHY I SAID YES TO 5-INCH HEELS FOR MY 13-YEAR-OLD

JESSA VARTANIAN AUBIN

Although I've never been one to read parenting books for advice, luckily, my older sister read a few when her sons were teens. So, when I texted her recently about my almost-15-year-old daughter wanting a second set of holes punched in her earlobes, a belly button piercing, and a dragonfly tattoo on her ankle, my sister texted me this sage advice: "Parenting teens = choosing your battles, letting them fail/make small mistakes so they can learn, but putting your foot down hard when it's too risky."

It reminded me of when this whole push–pushback dynamic with my daughter Avy began. It was about two years ago, when she got a $40 gift card to DSW for her 13th birthday. I instantly recognized that gift card as a precursor to battle, as Avy and I had been arguing over the "appropriateness" of sky-high heels for quite some time. (You can imagine which side of the argument I was on.)

I avoided requests to visit DSW for as long as humanly possible, but late August rolled around and I couldn't dodge back-to-school shoe shopping any longer. "Remember, we're here for tennis shoes," I reminded my daughter. Avy quickly picked out a pair of Nikes. Then she disappeared. My husband and son, also in tow that day, naively headed toward the cash register. I began an aisle-by-aisle search.

Eventually, I found Avy. She was sprawled on the floor in the clearance section, tenderly strapping on five-inch, sling back cork wedge sandals with thick black straps, gleaming gold buckles, and a small round peep toe. Not my style, and certainly not my preference for my 13-year-old, but one glance at her dreamy expression told me everything I needed to know.

"Do. Not. Say. A-n-y-t-h-i-n-g!" my daughter grinned mischievously when she spotted me above her. I watched as she carefully stood and edged toward the full-length mirror. She began to preen.

Granted, heels weren't a new obsession for Avy. She'd been infatuated since Christmas two years prior when my sister-in-law wrapped up a pair of shiny black, six-inch peep-toe stilettos that her daughter had been enthralled with at Avy's age. When Avy opened the box, I'm pretty sure she heard angels singing.

"OMG! I LOVE them! I look AMAZING!" Avy declared as she clicked across our hardwood floors in her new kicks. "I'm wearing these out to dinner tonight!"

"No, you're not," my husband and I chorused in response.

"Give me three good reasons why not!" our master-negotiator-since-birth retorted.

My husband shot me a "WTF?!" look—a look that failed to evaporate when I confessed I'd pre-approved the gift. I thought they would be a harmless tool for dressing up around the house, but now I realized Pandora's box had been opened.

My husband and I harmonized a whole slew of arguments around the notion that the shoes weren't appropriate, risked broken ankles and ripped tendons, and anything else we could come up with in the moment. When those arguments failed, we found ourselves resorting to words like cheap, easy, wrong impression—even explaining about ladies of the night, for god's sake. We were in deep now.

But if I'm being honest, I felt conflicted. While I certainly did not want my preteen leaving the house in stripper heels, I was having trouble making a solid case against it. She wasn't going out naked. It wasn't illegal. They were simply high heels, right? Maybe this was just a 'rite of passage' that a girl with a love of fashion needed to make.

Ultimately, I gave our 11-year-old the go-ahead. And she did wear those stilettos out of the house. Twice. Once, out to dinner, and once, to see a play in the city.

On both occasions, she got a few quizzical looks. Mostly, though, she got kind-hearted comments from grown women who enjoyed her spirit, admired her confidence, and who commiserated when she admitted the shoes were a bit painful—but totally worth it. I could almost see her self-confidence growing as she felt support, approval, and acceptance from her fellow females.

Now we found ourselves in the clearance aisle of DSW facing the same decision two years later. My husband asked me incredulously, "Are you really going to let her buy those?" Stuck in the middle of two opposing parties, I kept silent as my husband shook his head and said he'd wait outside for us.

As I explained to my husband later, I told our 13-year-old daughter yes because I saw the look on her face as she preened in that full-length mirror. She was gazing at her face, not her feet. She was seeing her future all-grown-up self, anticipating all the possibilities on her horizon. She was brimming with confidence, reveling in her own beauty. How could I not want to encourage that self-love and acceptance that so many women lack?

I said yes because, for several years, Avy had been lamenting how much she hates being "too old" for the little-kid fun stuff, but "too young" for the grown-up fun stuff. Somehow those cork wedges gave her hope that she wouldn't be stuck in limbo forever.

I also said yes because it was her birthday money, and she should be allowed to make her own choices.

I will admit that walking around the mall beside my 13-year-old in five-inch platforms made me a little self-conscious at first. Part of me wondered what the "other moms" were thinking, if they were judging me for letting my daughter strut around in shockingly high shoes.

On the other hand, while Avy knew her platforms were a tad inappropriate, she's always prided herself on going against the flow, which is a trait I admire and encourage.

But here's the best part, the part I totally didn't anticipate. Those wedges created an unexpected bonding experience. Moseying along beside my suddenly-5-foot-10-inch teenager, we couldn't help but giggle as she occasionally reached out to steady her gate. I tried to keep a straight face as she threw her arm over my shoulder, reveling in the newfound exhilaration of temporarily being taller than me. When I rolled my eyes at her (swapping roles briefly), she laughed and so did I. And it brought this mom and that teenage girl even closer.

As for that second set of holes Avy — almost 15 now — asked to punch in her earlobes last month? I said yes. She grinned wide at my yes and instantaneously begged to pierce her belly button at the same time, citing efficiency. I stood firm on that for now: Nope. We've also mutually agreed to postpone further arguments about tattoos until she's 16 (which of course she knows I won't let her do until she's 18).

Push.

Pushback.

The dance continues.

Before being sucked into the tornado of kid-raising, Jessa Vartanian Aubin published dozens of first-person essays in places including Runner's World, Cosmopolitan, the Los Angeles Times, and regularly contributed to a San Jose Mercury News column where she wrote endlessly about looking for love. Married with two kids and a dog now, she is finally emerging from the funnel cloud after a 10-year-absence and starting to string words together again. Find her on her website https:// www.jessaaubin.com/

HOW TO EQUIP OUR TEENS TO LIVE A GODLY LIFE

CHRISTINE CARTER

Note from the editors: This section of the book is about teaching our children values and value systems. We wanted to include religion as one of those value systems, for the parents who are trying to teach their children to live a Godly life. This essay takes the Christian point of view from the perspective of the author, but does not necessarily reflect the views of all contributors to the book.

Parents raise their kids with one final goal in mind -- to prepare them for independence. As our kids enter adolescence, the reality of this truth begins to sink in. We can become submerged in fears and worries of the great unknown as our teens begin to break away and we are forced to let go. The high school years resemble the airport runway as our kids to gain velocity and take flight.

How can we instill an unwavering faith in their hearts before the launch? How do we prepare our kids to reflect a God-like character in their ever-expanding world? How do we ensure our kids will make decisions according to our Christian core values?

As much as we want to keep them in the confines of our control, we need to set them free slowly. Rigid religion does not birth authentic faith, but rather sets them up to fail, or worse yet, rebel and walk away from God entirely. I propose we help them nurture their own personal relationships with Christ, which is above all, what Christians desire most for our kids. If they experience this intimate connection, we can trust that spiritual growth will occur and they will embark on their evolving path with the faithfulness we desire for our kids.

Here are eight important areas we can build the groundwork of our teen's faith and equip them to live a Godly life.

1. Understanding the value of their worth in God's love.

I praise you because I am fearfully and wonderfully made;
your works are wonderful,
I know that full well.
Psalm 139:14NIV

This verse (and the entire Psalm) encapsulates a truth we want our children to believe as they continue to develop their identity and learn more about who they are and how they fit into this world. As they face increasing pressure to conform and meet all the cultural expectations, remind them of this scripture. Their worth is not measured by what others think of them or how they perform. They are created with a unique design and purpose, fully whole, fully loved and accepted by God. His works are wonderful.

2. Accepting the profound unconditional grace in Christ.

As our kids meander through their own challenges, conflicts, and trials, it's important for them to know God will not walk away from them. As they inevitably face hard decisions amidst the unyielding stressors of adolescence—we want them to always feel the comfort and peace in knowing when they make mistakes—they are forgiven and there is always hope for redemption. Our kids don't need a punitive and punishing God in their lives. If they fear God's wrath or believe God is distant and unreachable unless or until they meet all required conditions...

They will believe in betrayal of the worst kind. And it's up to us to change that narrative and remind them constantly that there is nothing they can do to separate them from the love of God.

For I am convinced that neither death nor life, neither angels nor demons, neither the present nor the future, nor any powers, neither height nor depth, nor anything else in all creation, will be able to separate us from the love of God that is in Christ Jesus our Lord.
Romans 8:38-39 (NIV)

3. Believing in God's purpose and practicing His principles.

Teenagers live in constant uncertainty. They are exploring new social circles, new interests, new ideas, new experiences, new goals and future dreams that can be exciting, but also overwhelming, scary, and confusing. They need assurance that

God has a purpose and a plan and a passion for their lives.

When we teach our kids the importance of practicing Biblical Christian principles - such as self-control, patience, modesty, humility, honesty, and abstinence, remind your teens that this is God's way of keeping them safe, whole, and secure in their relationship with Him. These may look like 'rules,' but they serve to protect them from harm and pave the path God designed for them. God wants what is best for our kids, and living out these values will not only strengthen their faith, but help them grow and live out God's purpose for their lives with integrity.

With my whole heart I seek you; let me not wander from your commandments!

Psalm 119:10 ESV

4. Being practical and positive about "Plugging in."

The online world is our teens' new playground. This territory is a vast and sometimes vicious terrain that can be dangerous and damaging to our kids' well-being, *but* it can also be a positive connecting platform giving our kids ample room to practice the principles of their faith. This landscape offers opportunities for our kids to demonstrate Godly character in how they interact with others and in choosing what they share in the digital world. Spending time on social media has become a critical part of our kids' lives. It's up to us to be in it with them and help them be vigilant in adhering to their Christian values.

But in your hearts revere Christ as Lord. Always be prepared

to give an answer to everyone who asks you to give the reason
for the hope that you have. But do this with gentleness and
respect,
1 Peter 3:15 NIV

The reality is we can't see all their activity online, but we need to be in constant communication with our kids about what they see, what they share, and who they interact with and follow. Talk to your teen about the dangers of the internet, set clear limits on their phone use, and regularly monitor his/her accounts.

5. Building a heart of compassion and respect for others.

As our kids' world opens to new people, new voices, new ideas and opinions, we must impart the value in loving others and respecting all people, despite any differences. Our faith calls us to treat others as we would want to be treated, and our kids need to practice this principle- especially with people they struggle to understand or may not like. This can be a challenging exercise in self-control and grace- both critical in reflecting the heart of Christ. We need to practice what we preach ourselves, in modeling how to handle difficult people and show restraint in negative interactions and discernment in prayerful decisions when conflicts with others arise.

Do to others as you would have them do to you.
Luke 6:31(NIV)

We also want our kids to develop compassion for others and serve those who have extraordinary needs. There is a powerful awakening when we expand our kids' view to see the profound lack of basic rights and life-giving necessities all around them. Serving the homeless, going on mission trips, and learning about the atrocities around the world can open their view and help them see beyond themselves.

6. Understanding that Prayer is essential.

Prayer is a critical piece to grow our faith. Help your kids develop good prayer habits so they can experience a deeper and more personal relationship with God. Make sure your family prays together on a regular basis and encourage your kids to pray aloud with you. Let them know there is no wrong way to pray. I pray with each of my kids on the way to school. It's been an integral part of my kids' day as we invite God into our day.

Prayer can bring our kids a sense of stability and peace in trusting God to guide their paths as they involve Him into all the details of their lives. Keep a prayer journal for your family to record prayer requests and review them to see how God has answered specific prayers. Acknowledging the different ways God has worked in their lives will build assurance in His presence.

This is the confidence we have in approaching God: that if we ask anything according to his will, he hears us.
1 John 5:14 NIV

7. Participating in Christian community.

Community is a critical part of our Christian faith and attending a church on a regular basis is a wonderful way to connect with others, get involved in serving, and study God's word.

During these years, faithful fellowship with peers can be the greatest opportunity for our teens' spiritual growth. Having them actively participate in a youth group will provide them with the support they need to live a Godly life. Our kids need a community of Christian friends and mentors who will help guide them, teach them, and grow them in their walk with the Lord.

And let us consider how we may spur one another on toward love and good deeds, not giving up meeting together, as some are in the habit of doing, but encouraging one another—and all the more as you see the Day approaching.
Hebrews 10:24-25 NIV

8. The importance of staying connected.

As we escort our kids through these tumultuous years, communication is a critical element in staying connected with them. Although they are growing more independent, they still need us to be present in their lives. Don't be fooled by their detached ways, but rather show interest in what they are doing, and always be available to them. Be watchful of their actions, their moods, their activities, and offer support and encouragement as much as you can.

Our kids need us to be on their side and know they have our trust and confidence in the path they are paving for themselves. They also need to be assured that they can come to us with their failures, their fears, their questions, as they develop their own perspective and explore new ideas about the world and how they see things. It's up to us to cultivate a relationship that allows our kids to approach us with tough topics, uncomfortable news, or decisions that conflict with our core values. Remember, this season is all about exploring possibilities, expanding their world and developing their identity. We simply need to graciously love them through it.

All these components are vital in establishing a strong faith foundation for our kids. We can do our best to build the groundwork, but ultimately, we must trust in God's will for our kids and secure our hope in His promises!

For I know the plans I have for you," declares the Lord, *"plans to prosper you and not to harm you, plans to give you hope and a future.*
Jeremiah 29:11 (NIV)

Christine Carter writes at TheMomCafe.com, where she hopes to encourage mothers everywhere through her humor, inspiration, and faith. You can also find her work on For Every Mom, Blunt Moms, Motherly, For Her, Sammiches and Psych Meds, Moms of Tweens and Teens, Your Teen for Parents, Mamapedia, Her View From Home, The Mighty, Grown and Flown, Huffington Post, MomBabble, and Scary Mommy. She is the author of "Help and Hope While You're Healing: A woman's guide toward wellness while recovering from injury, surgery, or illness."

LITTLE WHITE LIES

SHANA MARTIN

Relating with tweens/teens can be difficult. One of the ways in which it is hard for me to relate to my 13-year-old daughter, Margaret, has to do with honesty. I am probably one of the most honest people you'll ever meet. This is partially because I place a high value on truth and integrity. And while I believe this is a trait that can absolutely be learned, I would be a liar if I didn't point out that I do believe nature has played a large part in this. Let me explain.

I was that child who never lied. OK-fine! I may have told a few white lies way back when I was a little kid, but overall, I told the truth. Either I was born without the ability to deceive others, or I had it in me to be a talented liar but had no interest in flexing that muscle.

Interestingly, my older brother, who is also one of the most honest people I know, was deceptive when we were growing up. I see that in retrospect, but somehow, I didn't recognize it when it was happening; I just remember him getting punished a lot.

A memory that sticks with me from my own teen years is being at the mall with my friends one day. We'd gone into a clothing store that had mannequins donning outfits that were so inappropriate for a teen, I would lock my daughters away for life if they wore them to school. When we were leaving the store, I noticed one of my friends hadn't paid for a belt she'd tried on, so I said, "Oh, don't forget to pay for the belt!" loudly. She and my other friend quietly escorted me away from the entrance, visibly annoyed at me. I was utterly confused until the lightbulb went on–she was shoplifting! I was stunned. And clueless. Stealing was the furthest thing from my mind. I was both impressed that she had the guts to steal and horrified that she would actually do it. (Update on those friends: they ended up turning out to be extremely honest and successful people to whom I hold in very high regard today. Double phew.)

Now that I've provided some context, let's fast forward around 30 years or so, to me as a parent to Margaret. I have joked in some of my blog posts about how adept Margaret is at being manipulative. Just as there is an element of thinly veiled truth in most jokes, in this instance, truth is naked. Unlike me, Margaret has a natural flair for being not-so-truthful. From little-girlhood through tween-hood and now teen-hood, she has used manipulation to try to get what she wants. She has omitted the truth to make herself look better. She has concocted stories to avoid getting in trouble. She has flat out lied to my face when I've called her bluff. And while I realize that (as was the case with brother and close friends growing up) some of this is par for the teenage course, it has still been a steep learning curve for me.

My husband has been a great teacher in this regard. As someone who shares Margaret's personality-type, he is much more equipped in dealing with her wily tactics. It's like he's got a device embedded in him that detects her bullshit. His approach is merciless preemption. Case in point: he regularly frisked her each morning in elementary school because she would stash all kinds of toys and personal belongings she was not permitted to bring to school in creative places. It was ugly. But necessary. And it worked.

To help Margaret be more truthful in all ways as she journeys through teenage-hood, I have communicated to her how much I value integrity, openness, and honesty as critical building blocks in my own relationships. She knows that to me, dishonesty is a huge turnoff–and can be a deal-breaker with a relationship. I would never turn my back on Margaret, but I've shared with her that trust is something sacred, and when you breach it, you can't easily build it back. So, each time she is not transparent with me is another withdrawal in the bank account of trust.

Margaret is aware of her not-so-truthful tendency and has really stepped up to try to address it. Thankfully, she is very receptive to what I share and seems to really take it to heart. She has a natural passion for learning, not just academically but emotionally as well. And she just cares so much about people and would never want to hurt anyone, least of all her family and friends. This gives me great hope! She realizes that hiding from the truth is not a healthy way to be.

We have been honest with Margaret that there is a fair amount of addiction in her vast family tree and that being able to honestly express one's self is a crucial component to avoiding the formation of bad and/or addicting habits. And I applaud her for this because at 13, I know that I had neither the self-awareness nor the insight required to do what she is doing at her young age.

To be fair, I have had to change some of my ways as a parent. My tendency to be completely open and honest is not always age appropriate. I have had to employ the duct tape parenting approach at times when I desperately want to share something with Margaret that I know she will think is funny, but resist because she's just not ready for that type of bonding. NOT easy!

If I can impart anything to Margaret about the importance of being earnest, I think this well-known quote sums it up aptly:

"Trust takes years to build, seconds to break, and years to repair." – Anonymous

Shana loves to spend time with her husband and two daughters, who are the truest sources of creativity, joy and personal fulfillment for her here on earth. Shana and her adolescent daughter, Margaret co-write "I Can't Relate Blog," a one-of-a kind blog about their unique perspectives on everyday life. In 2016, Shana published her first novel, Bequeathed, on Amazon. The story was inspired by the life of her maternal grandfather, an immigrant from Sicily. Shana has an MBA and has worked in a variety of industries over the last 23 years, including high technology, education, and healthcare. She currently works as a freelance business writer and has taught as an adjunct business instructor at two community colleges in Southern California since 2009. You can find her at https://martinstrategicprose.com

PART 4
THE EXPERTS WEIGH IN

We asked for input from counselors, therapists, youth workers, and legal experts to provide some advice on key areas such as communication, keeping our kids safe online, engaging with kids, and making them feel valuable and loved, and how to keep ourselves sane while we're dealing with the raging teen hormones and 'tudes.

TO AN ADOLESCENT, THERE IS NOTHING IN THE WORLD MORE EMBARRASSING THAN A PARENT.
— DAVE BARRY

RAISING LOVABLE, VALUABLE, AND CAPABLE TEENS

LINDSAY SMITH, LCSW

When we know that we are lovable, we know that we are worthy of giving love to ourselves and others; as well as receiving love from ourselves and others. We do not have the capacity for hate when we give and receive love fully. We are kind, compassionate, gentle, and forgiving with ourselves and with others.

When we know that we are valuable, we know that we have inherent worth and value. We value the worth of others. We don't cut others down; rather, we build one another up and support one another. We speak kindly to ourselves and others, we value our time and the time of others, and we are respectful of ourselves and others.

When we know that we are capable, we can be and do anything we want. We don't say to another, "You can't do that." We follow our passions and achieve our dreams and encourage the same in others.

When we live from a place of knowing we are lovable, valuable, and capable, everything is possible. Fear or doubt does not stop us. We are without internal limitations. We are happier, more confident, and more successful in both business and relationships. This is why it is imperative that we raise our children to know they are lovable, valuable, and capable, and to treat themselves and others as lovable, valuable, and capable.

Great! Now, how do I accomplish that?

Model Treating Yourself as Lovable, Valuable, and Capable

Teens see and hear everything we do. They may not show you they are watching and listening, but they are. You may think because they are rarely around or because they have their headphones on or are playing on their phone that they are oblivious to what you are doing; but that is not the case. In every aspect of our lives, the actions we model are teaching our teens how to behave - towards themselves, towards the family, and towards others.

The most important way to teach your teens that they are lovable, valuable, and capable is for you yourself to know you are lovable, valuable, and capable and to treat yourself and others in this way. If you do not know this for yourself, you will not be able to teach your teens. Not only that, but you will model the opposite to them and your teens will internalize that they too are not lovable, valuable, or capable.

If you tell your teens that they are lovable but later you mention you don't like your stomach rolls or you can't believe you forgot about a presentation at work and they see you beating yourself up about it, you are essentially saying to them, "You are lovable, but I am not." Your teens will not believe you. Why would they believe that they are lovable, if you, as their parent, do not believe that you are lovable? You get to show them you

146

love yourself by first, truly loving yourself, and then by showing yourself kindness and compassion and being gentle and forgiving with yourself. If you model this, your teens will see this and will learn that they, too, are worthy of loving themselves and treating themselves in this kind way.

If you stay in an abusive relationship or say that you knew your friend wouldn't return your phone call because she doesn't care about your friendship or if you do not have your own dreams or passions, you are modelling to your teens that you do not believe you are valuable. Again, if as adults we do not believe in our own value, why would our teens listen to us tell them they should value themselves? Why would they believe us when we tell them they can be and do anything they want? You get to show your teens that you value yourself by knowing you are worthy of being treated well and by taking safe and appropriate steps to change the situation if you are not being treated well. You get to show your teens that you have dreams and passions, that they matter to you, and that you believe that you can achieve them. When you model you are valuable to your teens, they, too, will get to see that they are valuable.

If you tell your teens you believe in them and you believe that they can accomplish anything they set their minds to, but do not follow your own dreams or talk about not having time to do what you really want to do, your teens will see that you do not believe in yourself or are not willing to do what it takes to accomplish your dreams. When your teens see that you do not believe you are capable, they begin to believe that they may not be capable either. However, when your teens see you pursuing your dreams and passions, even at a very slow pace, they begin to believe that if it is possible for you, then it is possible for them. You get to model that you are capable so that they can believe that they are capable.

If you do not currently know you are lovable, valuable, or capable, please take the time right now in your life to learn this. You may choose to visit www.iamlvc.org for support in this. Make this a priority in your life; it's an important step if you want to raise teens who know they are lovable, valuable, and capable.

If you already know that you are lovable, valuable, and capable (LVC), and you treat yourself and others as such, congratulations! That is a huge accomplishment and you are well on your way to raising teens who know they are LVC. The following sections include additional ways to support your teens in knowing they are LVC so they can treat themselves and others as LVC too.

Talk with Your Teens

Talk with your teens about why you believe it's important for them to know they are lovable, valuable, and capable and why it's important for them to treat both themselves and others in this way. The most impactful way to do this is by giving them examples.

You might share that when people love themselves they are kind to themselves and forgiving to themselves. When someone doesn't do as well on their math test as they had hoped, loving themselves may look like saying something to themselves like, "I studied hard for this test. I didn't do as well as I had hoped, but I will continue to study hard and do my best." You may also want to share with your teens that in truly loving them-selves they also seek to treat others with love. This might look like a friend talking really negatively to herself after a breakup and then saying something to their friend like, "I am here for you. I know this is difficult. I also know that you are worthy of a relationship where you are loved and treated well. And you are always worthy of loving yourself and being kind to yourself, even when you are going through hard things."

You may explain that when people value themselves they believe in themselves and they know they have inherent worth. When a friend changes plans at the last minute, this might look like saying something to themselves like, "Just because my friend has different priorities at this moment, does not di-minish our friendship or my value." Your teens may show they believe others are valuable by including someone who may feel left out or by encouraging a friend to know their own worth de-spite difficulties with peers or parents.

You may say that when people know they are capable, they believe they have the ability to be and to do whatever they want. They believe they can figure out how to make those dreams a reality. When someone knows they are capable and are told they won't be able to do something, they may say to themselves, "I know that I can achieve my dreams. I may not know exactly how I will do it yet, but I know I have the ability to figure it out." Your teens may show they believe others are capable by saying something like, "I know you can do this" and even point out a relevant skill when a friend expresses doubt in his/her abilities.

As you are talking with your teens about knowing they are lovable, valuable, and capable and treating themselves and others in this way, encourage a discussion. Ask them questions about how they have treated themselves or others in these ways in the past. You may also want to ask them how they have seen others treat themselves or others in these ways in the past. The more of a conversation this is, versus simply a one-sided lecture, the more your teens will internalize these beliefs.

Encourage Your Teens to Choose Self-Love

Share with your teens that loving themselves is a choice. They can choose to think negatively about themselves and their bodies as many of their peers will. They can choose to say things to themselves like "I look fat" or "She'll never want to talk to me" or "I'm stupid." But share with your teens that even if their friends are talking to themselves in this way, there is an alternative. They can choose to think positively about themselves and their bodies and they can choose to say things to themselves like "I am kind" or "I know I can do this" or "I love myself." Share with your teens what their lives might look like if they choose to love themselves versus not loving themselves:

Example of life when you don't love yourself: When you don't love yourself, you often feel down. You may say things to yourself like "No one likes me," "I'm never going to find good friends," or "My friends all have better bodies than me" and then you often feel lonely, sad, or discouraged. You may choose to hang out alone even though you want to be with friends. Or you may choose to hang out with friends, but then compare yourself to them and feel inferior. You may sometimes even feel like your life is not worth living.

Example of life when you do love yourself: When you love yourself, you know that your life is worth living. You are kind and compassionate to yourself. You may say things to yourself like "I love that I am a unique individual," "I know I will make mistakes and I choose to learn from them," or "I am thankful for my body and all it can do" and you will often feel joy, gratitude, and a sense of connection. Sometimes you will choose to hang out with friends and you will enjoy this time together, knowing you are each unique individuals. Sometimes you will hang out alone and will enjoy this time too. You will truly love yourself and value all that you are able to be and do.

If your teens want to make the decision to love themselves, have them try this exercise:

1. Make your choice and declare it. Close your eyes and sincerely, genuinely tell yourself that you are making a choice to love yourself truly, deeply, today and forevermore.

2. Stand in front of a full-length mirror, look into your eyes with love in the mirror, and say "I love you" to yourself over and over and over again until you can feel love in every inch of your body—from head to toe!

3. Throughout the days, weeks, and months ahead, every time you have a negative thought about yourself or your body, stop and say to yourself, "I don't think like that anymore. I love myself," and allow yourself to feel that love. In the beginning, you may end up doing this every 30 seconds or every few minutes. Just keep doing it. It will get easier and easier and the negative thoughts will

begin to come less often over time.

You may want to share daily with your teens something you said or did for yourself to show yourself love and ask them something they said or did to themselves to show themselves love. For example, you may share that you showed yourself love today when, after saying something you wish you hadn't said to a co-worker, you first apologized to the co-worker and then, rather than internally berating yourself, you told yourself, "I am thankful I realized my mistake and was able to apologize. I am choosing to be kind, compassionate, and forgiving to myself. I love myself." Your teens may share that they showed love today by choosing to walk away from a group of friends who were gossiping or by writing a list of 25 things they love about themselves. Encourage them to be in the habit of talking about how they love themselves, rather than how they do not love themselves.

Empower Your Teens to Know They Matter

Empower your teens to know that they matter. People sometimes feel as if they are not important or do not matter. This may be because of the way people have treated them, either through things they have said or done to them in the past. The truth though, is that you matter, your teens matter, every single one of us matters. Empower your teens to know that they are loved, they are valuable, and they matter.

Teach your teens that even when people do or say unkind things to them, it does not mean that they deserved this treatment. It is not a reflection of their value. When people do or say unkind, mean, or even abusive things, it is usually because they do not feel good about themselves, rather than because of something your teens said or did.

Author and motivational speaker, Jack Canfield teaches us to say, either inside our head to ourselves or aloud to others, "No matter what you say or do, I am still a worthwhile person." When your teens can understand this, they will not internalize another person's negative statements or actions. Teach them this now and encourage them to say this every single time someone does or says something to them that they do not like. This will help your teens become stronger and more resilient.

However, if something has happened in the past that your teens internalized, they may have developed negative thoughts about themselves based on these events. They may say things to themselves like, "You should have known better" or "You are so dumb" or "No one will ever like you now". These negative thoughts cause them to relive these past painful events on a regular basis.

Help your teens to not let the past steal one more second of their presents and futures. Have your teens write a list of the negative thoughts they have. Then have your teens identify at least five thoughts that they would like to have about themselves each day, such as "I am valuable" or "I matter" or "I am a kind and loving person". Each time your teens notice one of the negative thoughts coming to mind, have them replace it with one of the thoughts they would like to have. If your teens are having trouble with this, you may want to have your teens work with a Cognitive Behavioral Therapist who can help your teens through this process.

Teach Your Teens to Embrace Failure

Teaching your teens to embrace failure will help your teens to know they are capable. Many people view failure as something negative. They may feel defeated or discouraged or inadequate. A negative view of failure can cause feelings of embarrassment, hopelessness, and shame and can cause people to believe that they are not capable.

You can teach your teens to view failure differently. You can teach your teens that failure is the road to success. The most successful people have failed repeatedly. What differentiates the successful people is that they keep trying. They know that failure ultimately leads to success. It is not possible to become successful without failures. Failure is how we learn. Children fail at walking many times before they learn to walk. They don't give up though, they keep trying for days, weeks, months—however long it takes!—but they ultimately succeed.

Teach your teens to embrace failure. When they fail, help them to look for something to learn from the situation. Encourage them to apply what they have learned and try again. If they fail again, continue this process over and over until they achieve success. And allow your teens to define success in whatever ways they choose.

When your teens learn to view failure as a learning tool and even seek difficult situations knowing that failure is initially likely, they will know that they are capable, and this positive view of failure will assist them in reaching success faster. It will also cause both you and your teens to be happier along the way.

Each night, you may want to ask your teens what they failed

at today and what they learned from their failure. This will help your teens learn to accept, embrace, and seek out failures as stepping stones on their way to success!

You *can* raise lovable, valuable, and capable teens. Simply by taking the time and effort to read this book, you are well on your way. Choose to love yourself, choose to know your value, and choose to believe you are capable. Model treating yourself and others in this way and you will be able to teach your teens to do the same.

Lindsay Smith is a Licensed Clinical Social Worker and the founder of I Am LVC. The mission of I Am LVC is to empower people to know they are lovable, valuable, and capable and to treat themselves and others as lovable, valuable, and capable. If you would like support in knowing that you are lovable, valuable, and capable, or if you are interested in supporting this mission, visit www.iamlvc.org.

Lindsay is also the founder of Teen Therapy Center of Silicon Valley and Family Therapy Center of Silicon Valley. These Centers are located in Silicon Valley in California and provide counseling to children, teens, adults, couples, and families. You can find more information about these Centers at www. teentherapycentersv.com and www.familytherapycentersv.com.

Additionally, Lindsay created a game called Talk About It! to enhance communication between teens and adults through fun and familiar card and dice games with a twist. To learn more about how this game can support you and your teens or to get this game, visit www.talkaboutitgames.com.

NAVIGATING THE GENERATION GAP WITH CO—CREATIVE COMMUNICATION

LAURA LYLES REAGAN

Rolled eyes, deep sighs, glares and the silent treatment may be part of your glorious teen as they pull away from you. Psychologists say, it's all a part of their individualization and differentiation from their family as they move into the world; but, it can be uncomfortable, disheartening and maddening. It is possible to support their growth, let go and enjoy them again even in this stage of development if we understand the different positions parents and teens occupy in the social order. Rather than a psychological view about development, perhaps a sociological view which highlights the different "cultures" of parents and can help.

My parent journey began with two distinct influences. My premature daughter had surgery for an intestinal birth defect just three days post-birth. Two months later she had a second surgery for the same thing. She didn't feed with a bottle until three months old. We did not know if she would live or die. She was finally able to come home at four months old, but the first year of life was full of therapy, doctor visits and other interventions. I learned to let go and throw "normal" out with the proverbial baby's bath water.

The second influence was my schooling in sociology. I learned that the institution of family could be seen as a function of society to impart societal norms. I learned that other cultures perform this function differently and still have healthy children. This open-mindedness along with my personal reality of coming to terms with my powerless self on the third day of my child's life, served me well as I entered adolescence with both my daughters. I tried not to take their behavior personally. I tried to see their development as a function of their struggle to find their place in the world. I began to apply what I knew about culture to their positions in the social order of things and compared it to my role as an adult. I adapted the sociological and anthropological definitions of culture to the roles parents and teens play.

Parental Cultural Norms

Parents want teens to be responsible for themselves and have a better life than they did.

Teen Cultural Norms

Social scientists have observed that teens create meaning from the world around them and work together to create their own interpretations. It even happens with complicated issues like racism and gender roles. But adults sometimes miss the messages of teen culture and its creative force because we are too busy imparting adult culture.

Generation Gap

Popular culture calls this breach between understandings and the generation gap. Since cars were invented and teens asked for the keys on weekends and had a separate time away from parents, **teens have been creating their own culture.** Rock and roll was born as a result! Today, teens create their own language, meanings and of course music. Teen culture is dynamic and ever-changing. It flies at the speed of the internet through social media. In other parts of the world, the generations are not so divided. While the amount of time spent with each other daily is greater in tribal cultures when compared to our own Western culture, are we doomed to be disengaged as parents and teens?

No! We have choices. We can co-create the relationships we want and need with our teens.

Co-creation 101

Co-creation is a sociological and business term about relationships. Each party in the relationship shares the responsibility for the relationship and is empowered to influence the relationship.

Co-creation does not mean, however, that parents surrender healthy power and control in the relationship. Not only does the law respect the power differential between parents and their children, but society does too. Parents have more experience than their children. All research demonstrates that teens still see their parents as their first role models and first point-of-contact regarding how to navigate the world.

Traditional sociology views the role of children and teens as passive recipients of social learning where the institutions of society such as family, school and church teach children about our culture's beliefs and behaviors. But that doesn't ring true, especially with teens.

As any new parent knows, children definitely influence the parent-child dynamic by expressing their needs. Babies cry. Parents feed them, pick them up, change diapers. That influence continues throughout the child's life, especially with teens.

Co-creation happens all the time unconsciously. Unconscious co-creation occurs when mom or dad decide it's not worth the battle to remind their teen for the third time to take out the trash and they do it themselves.

But conscious co-creation occurs when parents build positive, effective relationships together with their teens by using open and direct communication skills with the focus on engaging and empowering their teens, rather than merely attempting to control their behavior. Teens can share full responsibility for defining and communication in the relationship.

Let's return to the unconscious co-creation trash example from above. What if mom said, "Joe, I'm really tired and it's an additional stressor for me to remind you to take out the trash since we agreed that would be your regular chore when we divided them up. What can I do to help you remember without being a nag?" That communication shares real emotion without blame and invites the teen to engage in problem solving without letting them off hook with the responsibility – a responsibility, they had a hand in shaping.

Examples of Co-creation

My youngest daughter loves horses. She has been riding since she was four years old. In her mid-teens, she discovered an approach of interacting with horses popularized by Monty Roberts, who is considered one of the first horse whisperers. He was made famous by the book, *Shy Boy,* which is the story of a wild mustang that communicated with Monty and followed him home. Mr. Roberts attributes this to the language of *equis.* It is the nonverbal communication horses use to communicate with each other. Mr. Roberts learned it over time and applied it to communicate with horses in their "language." By learning horses' language and behaviors, a human can interact with a horse in a way that invites partnership instead of submission to control and domination.

Parent and teen cultural communication is like that! When parents and teens understand the motivations of each and communicate in a way that is understood by both, positive things can happen that facilitate movement toward responsible adulthood in teens.

The following conversations show how the different roles of parent and teen can clash or effectively relate. The first is an unconscious conversation which many of us, as parents, know all too well. The last conversation is a conscious conversation using effective communication skills which reflect the understanding that teens are parents play different roles in society and therefore in the family and will see the world differently also.

Kim is a punk rocker in a town with no punk rockers. She

identifies with the "be your own person," rage against the system lyrics. She is tall, thin, beautiful and has soulful deep blue eyes. She has punk cut, blue hair and feels most at home in a mosh pit. Even though her hair and look scream, "pay attention," she is quite shy. Music helps her cope with her parents and stepparents. Yes, stepparents. She is sick of hearing about her clothes from her stepmother and her loud music from her stepfather. What do they know anyway?

Unconscious Conversation: Kim's Clothes Battle

Stepmom: So, what were you thinking of wearing to Emily's (older stepsister) wedding?

Kim: I want to wear that simple black dress you bought me last fall. I can accessorize it.

Stepmom: No! You don't wear black to a daytime wedding. I know you! You will want to

wear combat boots with it.

Kim: Yes! And black nail polish and dark eye and lip make up (with a sarcastic tone).

Stepmom: No! I forbid it. Wait till your father hears about this.

Kim: Fine. I just won't go.

An attitude of co-creation can best be conveyed by using effective communication skills that invite teens to engage in personal responsibility for the relationship with us. These communication skills are often the skills we use as adults in the workplace. By modeling these skills inside the teen – parent relationship, parents can prepare teens for the future. Communication skills include the following.

Open-ended questions can't be answered with a simple yes or no. They are used to invite full participation.

Active listening reflects the emotion and meaning of the communicator by the listener. It is used to confirm understanding or seek more information.

I-Messages use the formula, I feel _____ about _____ (behavior or belief). It demonstrates personal responsibility for your own actions, thoughts and feelings. Parents can also share meaningful messages this way.

The following conversation reflects an attitude that is essential to co-creation, non-judgmentalism. Neither Kim, nor her stepmom are "right." They simply have different perspectives because they occupy different positions in society as parent and teen. In the conversation below, both Kim and her stepmom have learned the communication skills through coaching sessions and are trying to use them. This is their attempt to work through a potentially conflictual situation.

Conscientious Co-creative Conversation:

Kim's Style, An Invitation and Open Mindedness

Stepmom: So, what were you thinking of wearing to Emily's wedding? Open-ended Question

Kim: I thought I would wear that black dress you bought me last fall and accessorize it.

Stepmom: Most etiquette books say that black for a daytime wedding isn't appropriate. How do you feel about a shopping trip to see what we can find?

Kim: So, you want to take me shopping because you don't

want me to embarrass you? **Active Listening Skill to Confirm Meaning**

Stepmom: No. I want to take you shopping because you need something new. You have grown since we went shopping last. **Clarification of Meaning in response to the Active Listening**

Kim: Ok. I'd like that. Thanks. But I don't think we will agree about what's appropriate. I feel disrespected when you "dis" my style. **I-Message**

Stepmom: I don't disrespect you Kim. We just don't agree sometimes about the appropriateness of your style. We will never know about a compromise dress if we don't go shopping and take a look at what's out there. Let's try to keep an open mind and try to find something that works for both of us. **I-Messages**

Kim: Okay.

Confession: My Purpose as a Parent

I am blessed to be the mother of two amazing adult daughters. Throughout their childhood and adolescence, I realized that attempts to control the behavior that I deemed problematic, either escalated the situation or shut down real relating. Many times, I fell short of using these communication skills. But I always celebrated when they used the skills on me! I was genuinely happy they were empowered even if it was hard to keep my cool or keep from laughing, depending on the circumstance.

I didn't see my role as authoritarian because they would not have the dignity of solving problems for themselves. Neither did I see my role as being their confidant, even though they opened up to me often. I saw my job as being a facilitator, to help them learn the skills they need for positive futures. None of us knows what the future holds for the next generation. The best we can offer them is a skill set to negotiate their own place in the world and contribute to others.

Coaching resources for better teen and parent communication can be found on my websites, LauraLReagan.com and Heart2HeartParents.com. Books that highlight the mindset or skills of conscious co-creative parenting include but are not limited to, Dr. Shefali Tsabary, The Conscious Parent, Parent Effectiveness Training and my own, How to Raise Respectful Parents.

Laura Lyles Reagan is a sociologist, speaker, teen and parent relationship coach and author of How to Raise Respectful Parents, www.LauraLReagan.com

PARENTS, CHECK YOUR EGO AT THE DOOR TO HAVE A BETTER RELATIONSHIP WITH YOUR TEEN

DARREN HORNE

My daughter was born in January 2016, and shortly after I was diagnosed with postnatal depression. I had no idea men could get this, and I arrogantly thought I could manage it myself. So, for most of 2016, I set about nearly destroying my business and family.

Near the end of the year, on the brink of totally losing everything to depression, I went all in on the fight back.

In hindsight, I can see that my ego was a big part of the problem. And ego is one of the things I see other parents battle with too.

Was ego one of the reasons I was diagnosed in the first place? Suddenly it was not all about me? I was not the center of attention, my needs were not important, and my skill base was inadequate. I had never held a baby before. I held my first doll during an antenatal class. I hated not being good at things or not knowing what to do, and I felt pretty much every woman was silently mocking my attempts to change nappies and dress my daughter.

And, as we all know, men hate to be laughed at.

But so do parents.

Because we know nothing. Really. I fear the day my daughter will ask why it rains, what the difference is between a goose and a swan, why Meerkats don't meow, or why broccoli doesn't taste like chocolate.

I am looking forward to doing those science kits, or mini bug adventure projects. Because I am going to get to learn WITH her. I have no idea what a woodlouse is! I don't know about different types of spiders!

And yet, because I have power, I have authority, I have responsibility - I think I know better. I see parents tower over their children using body language, and sometimes shouting to intimidate, because they are so afraid that their children will see through them.

"To intimidate."

When you held your son or daughter in your arms, did you think "I will use intimidation to make sure he or she does what I think is right."

I am also a media lecturer and have been teaching 16- to 19-year-olds for almost 10 years, and I have seen the impact of this kind of parenting. I have heard parents tell their children they should be lorry drivers, because they had a good career doing it. Minimalizing the potential their child has and crushing their self-esteem.

My advice when dealing with teens? We need to back off as parents. The first two or three decades of our life have no relevance any more. You are preparing your child to live and work in 2040 and beyond. Do you have any idea what that really looks like?

How will we communicate? Will everything be virtual reality, or augmented reality? Which dystopian or utopian film has it the closest? The way we date, learn, create, connect, and fall in love may well be very different. We won't need to worry about our children coming home with tattoos, they are more likely to have some form of enhancement, via implants or cybernetics.

As parents, we cannot impose our view of the world, our out-of-date education, and our wish for "things to be like they used to be" on our children.

Staying Positive

Words are magic. They are spells.

You can say "The music you listen to is rubbish". You can do that. It's a choice. You can say you hate the movies your children love. LOVE.

You can say "Gaming is bad, or a waste of time," because you don't game.

You can disagree with a career path and say "There is no money in it," but really, the jobs our children will be doing might not even exist yet.

You can say that you "Don't understand social media, and it is a bad influence" and you can position yourself in opposition to it.

But what you are really doing is creating walls and conflict between you and your child. Don't you remember what it is like when a parent mocks or dismisses something you love? It probably still happens to you now. In your thirties or forties, your parents still can pull down your enthusiasm, or to make you falter. Are there things that you, as an adult, keep from your parents because you can't be bothered to hear that negative feedback, or have conflict? Will your sons or daughters keep things from you?

Communication is so powerful, and there are things you can do to have a strong relationship with your children. The two most powerful are to keep your ego in check, and to try and stay current.

You Are A Leader

If you communicate in any way at all, you are having an influence, and that influence makes you a leader. We lead through our words, our silence, our actions, and our inaction.

Parents know this. Our children watch what words we use, how we put on our clothes and makeup, how we cook, how we treat other people, and in particularly how we manage our emotions.

Emotional intelligence is key, as the lack of it is one of the key factors contributing to the rise of mental health issues. But Stoic philosophy is also on the rise, and realizing that we are responsible for how we react to external factors is essential. We also color those events. So if your teenager has a messy bedroom, is that really a reason to feel angry? What caused that emotion? Is it actually a worry about what other people might think? Or that it's somehow disrespectful to you? Is it really that big of an issue, as long as they are happy and healthy?

Likewise, I try to do the same with my students. They do not arrive late, or not come in at all, or fail to hand in work, to spite me. It has nothing to do with me, that's my ego talking. It is no reason for me to have an emotional response. It has to do with their development, hormones, brain chemistry, and lifestyle.

Leaders don't keep score and they don't worry about what others think. They are happy to be authentic and vulnerable.

Ask Questions

Curiosity, compassion, and courage. That's all you need. Whether we like it or not, parents are life coaches, so we need to help our children work things out for themselves. Asking open and non-judgmental questions can really help. So for clarity ask, "In what way?" Or to dig deeper, "And what happens then?" Another great one is, "What would you like to have happen?" This can often be followed by, "And what needs to happen for X to happen?"

Try it and see what happens.

Words are a terrible way to communicate. Put your ego aside, manage your emotions, and have the courage to realize you do not necessarily know best, or that you understand what your child is even saying. And have enough compassion to get at the truth. Your child will benefit tremendously from this humility on your part.

Darren Horne is an Educator / Consultant / Motivational Speaker / Author & Writer / Media & Communications Specialist. His daughter was born in January 2016 and he developed post-natal depression and soon realised he had been struggling with anxiety and depression his whole life. The fight back was intense, but he learned many skills and techniques to manage it. He realised that he, like many, had been living a life of fear, staying on the sidelines instead of chasing our dreams. His mis-sion is now to help make the world a better place and encourage others to go from farm boy to Jedi. Learn more about Darren at: http://darrenhorne.com/

KEEPING TEENS SAFE ONLINE — A PROSECUTORS PERSPECTIVE

EMILY BAKER

"What are you going to tell your kids about being safe online?"

I get this question a lot...like, A LOT. I can't blame them; people want to know what a former Prosecutor is going to tell her kids. I spent over ten years as a District Attorney with the Los Angeles County District Attorney's office, and this experience gives me a unique perspective into the kinds of things people get up to online (and elsewhere but that is for another day). I believe that kids need to be told honestly about the benefits and pitfalls of being online. The world our kids are navigating is completely different than how most of us experienced out teen years. Heck I didn't have a cell phone until after I graduated from college.

Technology has made access instant. You can pretty much connect to anyone or anything, anytime from a mobile device. For parents this makes the job of keeping kids safe online even harder. Gone are the days of just searching the family computer for its internet history and cookies. It is easier than ever to hide the activity on your phone using private browsing and apps designed to hide information from prying parental eyes. The 'online' world as it applies here involves more than just searching the internet, social media is a dynamic factor in this conversation. Because what is happening in the virtual world is more than just stumbling across some nudity.

Kids are sexting, kids are becoming addicted to internet porn and internet games that simulate gambling. Kids are sharing nude photos of themselves and others, which opens them up to criminal prosecution. Kids are being groomed as victims to be abducted into sex slavery and human trafficking. It is a very diverse landscape.

Not only are kids victimized online in different ways, they are also getting themselves in legal trouble in ways that weren't even conceived of years ago. A 17-year-old girl in Massachu-setts was recently convicted of involuntary manslaughter and sentenced to 2 1/2 years in prison for texting her boyfriend encouraging him to kill himself. This is the first time someone has been found criminally liable for another person's suicide. The words that are said, the pictures that are shared can have tremendous consequences.

Let me repeat that: *The words that are said, the pictures that are shared can have tremendous consequences.*

Unfortunately, you can't have a conversation about keeping kids safe online and on social medial without talking about sui-cide. According to CDC data from 2014, suicide is the second most common cause of death for age groups 10-34. The first cause is unintentional injury including accidents. As suicide rates continue to increase each year, more research is being conducted to see how social media and internet usage plays into this. The most recent and one of the most shocking examples of this comes from Russia. An app called "Blue Whale" has been linked to 130 teen suicides. This app uses techniques to get teens to complete challenges, the final challenge is killing yourself. This exists! One of the hardest things for parents to combat is that most of the apps kids are using are introduced to them by their friends.

So, what do I tell my kids about being safe online? I tell them the truth because it is really the only option. We can only shield our kids for a short period of time because eventually they will have to learn to work with the technology that our world demands. Is anyone else in a school district that requires iPads and assignments turned in online starting in 6th grade? It is our job as parents to teach kids the choices they will have to make, the consequences that are out there and the potential harm. Kids will have to learn to self-regulate and make good choices. Because eventually they will be without our guidance, and that will come faster than we anticipate.

How do we approach this? My approach is four parts that you need to remember. Trust, Talk, Try, and Tell.

Trust.

This is not as much about you trusting your child, but about them trusting you. Your kids have to trust that when they tell you what is going on you aren't going to judge them, flip out on them, or shame them. They need to know that when it comes to them being in over their head you are going to be there for them, that there is nothing that would cause you to abandon or forsake them. This sounds crazy to you ... you are thinking "Of course I wouldn't turn my back on my child when they are in trouble, scared or have made a bad choice. Of course I will love them even if I am disappointed." I am telling you this because I have seen it. I have seen good kids from loving families be pulled away from their parents. I have seen kids get assaulted and then told by their assailants that their families won't love them anymore because of what they have done. It sounds so bizarre, but it works. People who victimize use isolation as a powerful weapon. *These predators make victims feel as if they understand them, that they care for them when no one else does.* They create a fake 'us against the world' bond ... a total Romeo and Juliet thing. Predators use that 'bond' to control their victims, then they will blackmail or shame their victims, "What would your mom think if she saw these pictures you sent to me, she wouldn't still love you, she doesn't understand you, she doesn't want us to be together, she is jealous of you, I love you, I am the only one here for you..." It's scary and it works.

My Suggestion - Trust first, then employ the same tactics. Trust yourself and trust your kids and pay attention to building a family bond with some of that 'us against the world' attitude. I don't suggest this is easy but having those little family rituals like a game night, or a yearly trip can go a long way. It doesn't have to be extravagant; it just has to be unique to your family. Prove to your kids that you are there for them by hearing them out, even when they are being irrational crazy people that push all your buttons. Try telling your kids when you are wrong, admitting mistakes can go a long way toward building trust. As kids get older start asking them to work with you, tell them where you are challenged and ask for their help. How this works practically will look different in every family dynamic and it may not be easy, but it is worth starting where you are and building those bonds.

Talk.

My oldest is nine years old as I write this. I want to shield him from the world. I don't want to have to talk about this stuff and I feel like he is too young, yet I know he isn't. I want him to still be a kid, yet he does have a cell phone. We set ground rules and boundaries around screen time and content, but he still fights with me because I won't let him play the app PixelGun that some friends are allowed to play on their iPads. It is super annoying to be asked 10,000 times if we can download this stupid game. So, I tell him the truth in the most age appropriate way I can. I keep telling him that PixelGun has a chat feature that allows strangers to contact him and I am not ok with it. I explain over and over that there are people online who pretend to be kids to make friends and then are either inappropriate or can try to get information about where you live, or where you go to school and that isn't safe. I remind him yet again that it is my job to look out for him, and not letting him play that app is part of my job. I told him that I will keep an eye on the app and when the chat feature is able to be disabled we will re-evaluate it, but for now the answer is no because I don't trust the other people. I always tell my kids that while I trust them, I don't trust other people.

As kids get older the conversation will naturally be franker. Ask them directly, 'Has anyone ever tried to chat with you who you don't know? Have your friends gotten any cool new apps that you are interested in?' This starts in 4th and 5th grade, if not sooner.

When kids get into Junior High and High School, getting them to talk can be more difficult but try to figure out what their friend group is up too. When I talk to High School students I am amazed by the struggles they have with this stuff. From people sharing nude photos around school to bullying on apps like BurnBook and BurnNote. Kids are more likely to tell you what other kids are doing so ask about that. At least then you know what is popular at your school and how kids are communicating with each other. If you aren't getting answers from your kid, you can always call or meet with your school resource officer. This is the police officer who is assigned to your school, they are a wealth of information and truly care about keeping kids safe.

We are the ones who must help our kids navigate this landscape and teach them to cope with the ups and downs of social media. We have to talk to them openly and honestly, so we can teach them how to deal with all that comes at them online. The trouble with social media is not simply internet predators, but the drama of social media. Who hasn't seen a group of friends out together on Facebook and felt left out and hurt. I am a grown ass woman and it still hurts my feelings, but to a teen... those hurts are more significant and harder to deal with.

Try.

Don't tell me 'but SnapChat is stupid and I don't get it.' You have to try it. You need to understand how these apps and services work. If your kid is open to talking about it, have them show you. If not, then find a parent buddy (I volunteer if you need one) and ask them to try these apps with you. Look at how messages can be sent and hidden. Figure out if the app shows your location, is it video or photo based, what are the privacy settings like. Look around as if you were test driving a car. Figure out the features and if you aren't sure how to use something, do what your kid would do. Check YouTube. If you are really curious do a YouTube search for how to hide texts from your parents. There are hundreds of videos with tens of thousands of views each.

Part of the challenge is figuring out what app's and services kids are using. Facebook is not where kids are because it's been taken over by the Pinterest generation of moms. So where are they...well some are on Twitter and Instagram but teens love privacy. So apps like SnapChat, and What'sApp are very popular. Teens also like Twitch, Peach (which is on the way out), Kik., and Omegle. Because this is a topic that people are starting to pay more attention to you can generally find updated lists as these things change.

Tell.

Along with having a parent buddy to try these apps with, tell other parents what you are learning. Social media has allowed us to be less isolated that other generations of parents. We are able to find information, connect with each other and find safe likeminded groups to communicate about the challenges of parenting. If you find an app is being used in your kids' school ask if others have heard of it. Talk to the parents of kids yours is hanging with. I contacted several parents about this Pixel-Gun app thing and asked them about the chat feature. Some parents said that the wi-fi on their kids iPads was turned off, so they weren't worried about it, some didn't know it existed. Approaching it made me feel a lot better and let me know where other parents stand.

I am a firm believer in community, either locally or online. If you have a community of parents with kids going through similar stuff it will make it a lot easier on you. You don't have to know everything, you don't have to have all the answers, you just have to know where to look.

Pro-Tip

If you are worried about your kid's behavior or their behavior has changed in a concerning way, trust your gut. It's ok to be 'that' parent when it comes to your kid. If you have checked their phone and online profiles and don't see anything remember to look for their 'other' accounts. Most kids have more than one social media account on multiple platforms. Yes, this is like password hell for us, but it is the regular for them. Finally, there are tons of resources online that can help you navigate the ever-changing digital world. You've got this.

A great list of resources for online safety including cyber bullying: http://endcyberbullying.net/online-resources/

Emily Baker has been a practicing attorney for 11 years, most of that was spent as a Los Angeles County District Attorney. After illness and injury Emily realized that she needed something different in her life and in 2017 she became the CEO of her life and founder of *Ask A Lawyer Now*. *Ask A Lawyer Now* provides affordable legal guidance and strategy when you need it.

Starting a web-based company was particularly appealing to Emily because she is a giant tech nerd. Emily loves all things tech and thoroughly enjoys biohacking. Fun fact, Emily is one of the first 80 Certified Bulletproof Coaches in the world and puts butter in her coffee every morning. This unique experience and knowledge makes Emily a sought-after contributor and speaker. Emily is a TedX speak and has been featured various media outlets including; The Good Life Dr. Oz Magazine, Woman's World Magazine, *Bulletproof.com*, *Boss-Mom.com*, *BravoTv.com*. Social

www.YouTube.com/EmilyDBakerEsq
www.instagram.com/EmilyDBakerEsq
www.Facebook.com/EmilyDBakerEsq

I THOUGHT I WAS A DECENT PARENT UNTIL I HAD TEENS

JENNIFER LAURENZA

Before I had kids, I imagined something semi-glamorous, where I would calmly respond to all my children's needs, form strong emotional bonds that surpassed all parenting standards, and, when they were older, have long, philosophical conversations about love, life, drugs, sex, and all things without a trace of anger, sarcasm, or disbelief. And no yelling. Ever.

I even imagined that I would remain perfectly balanced as a person, staying trim and fit, pursuing educational and career goals (a Ph.D. before age 30? No problem ... so I thought) and maintaining excellent self-care consistently throughout. I had this parenting thing figured out. I was going to kick some serious parenting ass.

And then I became a real-life parent. My expectations have shifted. Keeping my children alive from infancy and beyond became the primary marker of success. I no longer judge parents with screaming toddlers or preschoolers in the grocery store—non-parents have no freaking idea what it's like to shop with three young children in tow, for the record. Having young children was physically exhausting. I wondered if I would ever sleep soundly again without a voice calling me from another room or a chubby face appearing next to mine in the middle of the night—scaring the living hell out of me. I wondered if the tantrums of my middle child would ever stop or if I would still be watching her at 16 years old throwing herself onto the floor every time she didn't get what she wanted. I caught sleep when I could, tried not to yell, and worked relentlessly at keeping the self-esteem of three girls intact through middle school while trying not to wish time away. When they became teenagers, I reasoned, things would be calmer, more relaxed, easier.

But parenting teens is an extraordinary feat that no one, to my knowledge, has ever quite captured in books, articles, movies, or even sitcoms. I have two teenage girls (ages 17 and 16) and a tween girl (age 12). I know from personal experience that there is nothing and no one (not even the so-called experts) that can prepare you for the transition from elementary school to middle school or from middle school to high school. NO ONE can prepare you for your sweet child turning into a raging ball of hormones, irritability, and lovability all at the same time. Throw in some serious stressors—like divorce, blended families, mental health issues, or medical problems and you have yourself a gigantic mess.

Childhood innocence is a thing of the past in my home. I don't know when my 12-year-old stopped hugging me so tight or stopped needing me to tuck her in at night, but it doesn't seem so long ago. In fact, she seemed to change from an innocent, sweet little girl to an angsty tween overnight. She used to follow me around and cling to me to the point where I felt almost suffocated, and now I am lucky to talk to her in between Facetime calls and Snapchat stories. I miss those times, suffocation and all. Seize the moment, they say. Each moment is constantly changing; I can attest to that.

Generally, I try to say yes more than I say no, unless it is inherently harmful or dangerous. That has been my parenting philosophy. As a result, I have made parenting decisions that I never thought I would make. I never imagined I would allow my teenager to get a belly button ring (or that my kid would even want one) but I did. I never thought I would let my tween dye her hair either, but I did that too. My 16-year-old walks around in her underwear and a shirt because she feels comfortable in this attire at home. Is this appropriate? I don't know. I have a house full of women and I have decided there are worse things.

Sometimes I feel like the butt of a few too many jokes because, apparently, I am not as cool as I thought. I always thought I would be one of the "cool moms," but frankly I think that is an oxymoron. I try to check my ego at the door (literally, when I walk in the front door) because teens and tweens are merciless in their honesty. And my kids are (mostly) kind and generous. But I am still their 40-year-old mother who wears ballet flats (no more heels for this aching back) and t-shirts when I am not working. Every assumption I have ever had has been challenged. I thought I was politically left until my 17-year-old daughter started engaging me in conversation and her anger at me was palatable. Now I feel like I am only slightly more left than a dictator.

When they ask if what they are wearing looks good, they do the exact opposite of what I say because ostensibly that's a clue as to what ACTUALLY looks good. I stopped expecting kids from age 11 and up to contribute at all to my self-esteem as a parent or as a person. It's a losing battle. Talking to other moms helps a lot with this. I feel a little less crazy and a lot more normal.

Just today, and several times prior, my 12-year-old daughter reminded me AGAIN that I am genetically responsible for her large breasts. This is YOUR fault, she said, as she tried on bikini tops in increasingly larger sizes. She was joking, and we laughed, but she was serious too. I get it. My own large breasts were unwelcomed at that age, too. But seriously—I carry enough mother guilt as it is. Am I responsible for my kids' breast sizes, too?

None of this is about me, I reiterate silently every day. Although some of it is. So, I try to screw them up as little as possible, with a whole lot of positive reinforcement thrown in as insulation. That's not much of a formula, but only two of my three kids are in therapy so far and I consider that a win. I try not to fall into the trap that Facebook and other social media offer since social media perpetuates the myth that your *friends'* families are perfect and angelic. We all know the truth. Each family is messy and glorious in its own way. We control the image we portray to the world.

I am a therapist by trade and I am considered by others to be an expert in my field. To my kids, I know practically nothing unless their friends say it's true OR another adult that they happen to admire agrees. Apparently, I talk funny, use outdated slang, fail to understand words like "lit" properly, listen to lame music, and have even worse taste in television or movies. We all have parenting fails, like the time I took my elementary-aged child and two tweens to a Keisha/Pit Bull concert. The tickets were free, and it seemed like a good idea at the time. Empathic failures will happen too, but a very wise friend told me that the empathic failures balance us out as parents so that we do not create self-involved, entitled monsters.

Some things I believe I have done well. For instance, I have done my best to create an honest and open relationship with my kids. I want them to be able to talk or ask me about anything. And mostly, I think they *do* talk to me. Not about everything, I am sure. Admittedly, sometimes they hate my advice and sometimes I give guidance when they just need me to listen. There are isolated moments where I long for the closed days of my childhood when certain subjects were taboo and parents didn't talk to their children about real stuff. Like the time my 15-year-old daughter nonchalantly asked me what a "chode" was—a term she had heard in school. I froze...temporarily. I seriously doubted my competence as a parent of teens in that moment. I was honest—I told her I had no idea but that I would research this immediately and get back to her. (If you don't know, a *chode* is basically a short, stubby penis.) I tried to mask my sense of incompetence with the internal voice that kept telling me, "It's better that she asks you than her friends or even worse, that she googles it herself." Let me tell you: the pictures I stumbled on when I googled that word were not meant for the eyes of a 15-year-old.

My favorite part of parenting burgeoning young adults is their idealism and optimism for the future. Without it, the world as we know it would be doomed since the rest of us have acquired some level of cynicism or bitterness along the way. It is our job to launch our adolescents into adulthood as prepared as they can be. This means that I need to let go of some things and ease them into this transition, which is in direct opposition to my natural inclination to protect (or overprotect) them from all harm. Hyper-vigilant or rigid parenting (the extreme of which is helicopter parenting) is not your friend. That's how you end up with rebellious kids or, on the opposite side, kids who live in your basement until they are forty because they are afraid of the world.

To keep myself sane, I engage in meaningful work, meditate as much as I can muster, write, and read. I try to commiserate and celebrate with other moms throughout this whole parenting gig because we all need that. Without that support, the isolation is suffocating. Parenting tweens and teens is a lot like life in general—you don't know what you are doing or where you are going, but the journey is sweet if you really pay attention and savor the positive parts … notwithstanding the migraines, weight gain, and gray hair experienced along the way, of course.

Jennifer Laurenza is a wife, a mother, and a Licensed Mental Health Counselor and Licensed Marriage and Family Therapist with a thriving private practice and wellness center. She is an advocate for the LGBTQ community and other marginalized populations. In the past sixteen years, she has carved out a career path that has included both clinical work and grant writing because of her passion for both. As a grant writer, she helped secure millions of dollars in federal, state, and private funding for nonprofit organizations. As a therapist, she strives to help people live meaningful and authentic lives. Jenn lives in southeastern Massachusetts with her wife, three daughters, two dogs, and four cats.

CONCLUSION

Perhaps you're in the throes of parenting tweens and teens, or maybe you have years to prep. Regardless, we hope you found the stories in this book to be entertaining, useful and a reminder that this new chapter can be fun too. Seriously, it can!

If there is one thing Alexa and I have learned over the years, there are many ways to parent. As moms, we each have our own style, gifts, personalities and dreams. While we love to pick up tips and tricks from others, we ultimately need to do what's best for our families. In fact, I often need to adjust my mom tactics for each of my kids. Who knew three beings coming from the same mom and dad could be so radically different? Just when I think I have it down, the younger two throw me a curveball.

Puberty, the push for independence, technology, drugs, driving – it scares us all. But the over-riding sentiment in every essay you read is one of love for our kids. Each phase of parenting brings its own unique set of challenges, but we endure. We've simply traded the years of potty-training and toddler tantrums with new trials of managing tech-obsessed teens, hormones and eye rolls. But, through it all, we love.

We love witnessing our kids' growth.

We love seeing their personalities emerge.

We love the forced family fun, the high heels, the armpit hairs, the cryptic texts and the quest to figure it all out.

It's simple. We love our kids. Even in the tween and teen years. Even when we think we might not survive the smells and sass and craze. We will. Because we love them.

SPECIAL INVITATION

Download your FREE copy of our 2nd Book: Lose the Cape: Never Will I Ever... (and then I had kids!) here ===> http://losethecape.com/Amazongift

We want you to be part of our Lose the Cape tribe! If you're interested in joining our Mom Squad group, we invite you to oin us here: https://www.facebook.com/groups/YourMomSquad/

If you write about motherhood and want to contribute to the Lose the Cape blog, please email us your submission at info@ losethecape.com.

Be sure to check out our podcast - we've been talking ALL about Teens lately, so lots of information for you at http:// losethecape.com/podcast or find us on Itunes or Stitcher.

Let's get social! Please follow us here:

Facebook: Facebook.com/LoseTheCape

Twitter at twitter.com/LosetheCape

Instagram: instagram.com/LosetheCape

Pinterest: pinterest.com/LosetheCape

Finally, if you've enjoyed this book, we hope you'll visit us on Amazon and/or GoodReads and leave us a raving review. This will help other parents find us too!

ABOUT THE EDITORS

Alexa Bigwarfe is a freelance writer, wife, mother of three children, and a dog owner. In addition to raising her children, managing her home, and writing, Alexa's heart is in advocacy and raising funds to support nonprofit organizations involved with infant, children and women's issues. Alexa launched her writing with her personal blog No Holding Back, (katbiggie. com). Here she chronicles topics including health and wellness, living with autoimmune diseases, and most importantly, her grief after the loss of one of her twin daughters to complications from Twin to Twin Transfusion Syndrome (TTTS). Alexa took the experience from that painful life event and channeled it into a compilation book for grieving mothers entitled *Sunshine After the Storm: A Survival Guide for the Grieving Mother*. In addition to the Lose the Cape series, she has been published in multiple other anthologies and several books on the topic of writing and publishing, including *Ditch the Fear and Just Write It!*. Alexa enjoys writing articles about parenting and children's health and wellness topics for regional parenting publications and podcasting about parenting, current events, and the actions of brave women who are changing the world. In her "spare" time, you can find Alexa enjoying time with her girlfriends or hiding in her closet for some "alone" time.

Kerry Rivera is a full-time working mom of three kids with a to-do list that stretches to "infinity and beyond." Between a demanding corporate gig, the nightly homework and kids' activities, and managing a household with her full-time working husband, she blogs about the "juggle" at BreadwinningMama. com. Her career journey started in the newsroom trenches and has since transitioned to working for one of the largest global automotive companies. She additionally writes for corporations, government agencies and brands in her "spare" time, and especially enjoys sharing the joys of modern parenthood around the web. Her love for content creation is only trumped by her love for content consumption. Her Kindle and nightstand are equally full, and a stack of magazines can be found in every room of the house. As a Southern California native, she takes advantage of the outdoors, enjoying both the beaches and mountains with family and friends, and loves to caffeinate with Starbucks Refreshers and Coke. She aspires to perfect a handstand in yoga, but is still working on touching her toes.

ACKNOWLEDGMENTS

We want to thank the contributors who were brave enough to share their voices for this book. As parents of tweens and teens, it can be tough to write about older kids. We recognize we need to respect their privacy, but we also love to share our stories. When you write about parenting, our kids get dragged into the mix. Thank you for sharing your laughs, your wisdom and your personal experiences.

We'd also like to thank our faithful, always honest and diverse Lose the Cape community. Thank you for engaging with us on the blog, in social media, for listening to our podcasts and for reading our books. We strive to create a space where all parents feel accepted and safe to share. Your energy, sense of humor and kindness are evident in every interaction we have with you. Truly, you are AH-MAZING! We love our peeps.

This book would have taken years more to complete had it not been for the help of our team. Nancy Cavillones, you keep us sane and on track and as organized as can be expected for two moms who have no capes! Adrienne Hedger—once again, your cover design knocked it out of the park! Michelle Fairbanks—the graphics were ON POINT! Thanks for taking Adrienne's incredible artwork and running with it. And Raewyn Sangari—

your support and social media expertise is a crucial part of our daily business. And Cheryl, thank you for your support on social media.

And finally, we would be remiss to not thank our families. You fuel our creativity. You drive us nuts. You make us laugh. You make us lose our minds as often as the capes, but we wouldn't have it any other way. Love you always.